What If... I'm Not Real?

A journey back to find the one I lost.

CHEYANN ROSE

BALBOA.PRESS
A DIVISION OF HAY HOUSE

Balboa Press books may be ordered through booksellers or by contacting:

Balboa Press
A Division of Hay House
1663 Liberty Drive
Bloomington, IN 47403
www.balboapress.com
844-682-1282

Because of the dynamic nature of the Internet, any web addresses or links contained in this book may have changed since publication and may no longer be valid. The views expressed in this work are solely those of the author and do not necessarily reflect the views of the publisher, and the publisher hereby disclaims any responsibility for them.

The author of this book does not dispense medical advice or prescribe the use of any technique as a form of treatment for physical, emotional, or medical problems without the advice of a physician, either directly or indirectly. The intent of the author is only to offer information of a general nature to help you in your quest for emotional and spiritual well-being. In the event you use any of the information in this book for yourself, which is your constitutional right, the author and the publisher assume no responsibility for your actions.

Any people depicted in stock imagery provided by Getty Images are models, and such images are being used for illustrative purposes only. Certain stock imagery © Getty Images.

Print information available on the last page.

ISBN: 978-1-9822-6121-4 (sc)
ISBN: 978-1-9822-6122-1 (hc)
ISBN: 978-1-9822-6293-8 (e)

Library of Congress Control Number: 2021901522

Balboa Press rev. date: 02/01/2021

Courage to Change

It takes great courage and inner strength to change from what is known and comfortable to something which is new and fresh. That which is unknown often contains our greatest potential. To seek our potential by risking change is the path of true greatness. Such action brings great favor and untold blessings.

—author unknown

To Spirit, the One who loves me as I am, has shown me who I am and to whom my life is devoted.

Contents

Preface

Do you remember who you were before the
world told you who you should be?

—Danielle LaPorte

*A*t my conception, those outside of who I am began to plan who
and what I was to be, and a personality was formed for me. Who
I am was to be ignored, unheeded, and unrecognized and to later
become unaccepted and rejected. "Who are you?!" were words I was
to hear as I transitioned from child to teen to adult—never fitting
in, never belonging, an outcast, for I did not, could not fit into the
box chosen for me. And yet the day came when I lost myself and,
with a personality not my own, formed in swirling thoughts of
increased fear, I unknowingly fell into that box that would keep me
captive having, by now, forgotten who I am and who I came here
to be. The lid was firmly closed, and I lived in the dark, unseeing
and hearing nothing but what echoed from thoughts given to me in
my box, bouncing back into me, to echo over and over again. And
this was all I heard—that is, until the day came when I knew I could
no longer survive within this dark, noisy container of personality
chosen for me and shouted out for help.

So very slowly, the lid opened, and light shone in, at first so blinding that I closed my eyes. Later, as my eyes adjusted, I took the chance to look around me at where I had been so long. What I saw was not what I had long been told to see, and perception by perception began to transform, become right side up, suddenly clear and so very different, so very lovely and the total opposite of the thoughts from which I had been birthed and had molded me to be. At first, I did not recognize this being in the box with me or know that she was me. Nor did I understand that the lid was now off this box that had long held me, and I could stand upright and even venture out when and if I was ready. When I finally had the courage to take that first peek over the edge, the world I saw was radiant and beautiful, and it was mine to walk free to be me.

Did I dare? Was I strong enough, brave enough to step out of this hated but secure box that I believed had kept me safe, for this is what I had been told?

It took time, but I didn't make one move without help, help that, by now, I knew was there all along with me inside this box. It was not only with me, but also in me as me and who I came here to be. Taking the hand offered to me, I took that first step outside the box and learned to stand upright. With faltering steps, I began to walk and explore this new life I had found. From walking, I began to run, as there was so much to discover, to see, to breathe, and to hear in this freedom I now found myself within. Soon, I found that I remembered much. From where, I had yet to remember. But it was familiar, it was delightful, and it was divine. Best of all, it was all mine to live within. Here, the true me emerged, laying aside the personality given to me to hide all that I was, all that I came to be—the real me to just be who I AM.

Introduction

*Honor the past as your teacher, honor the present as
your creation and honor the future as your inspiration.*

—Jamie Sams and David Carson

This is a two-part story of my life. The first, memories of what I
thought I lived. The second, the truth of what had really happened.
Within each chapter, both are shared—the memories and the truth
divided by a sword. This sword is the Sword of Truth that sliced
through the darkness of a frightened mind, allowing in light so that
I could see the truth of each person, each experience and to reveal
the lessons held that I could not see in the dark. Each lesson, finally
seen, revealed to me what I had forgotten long ago and, thereby,
helped me remember who and what I am in truth. It was here I
found the one I lost and who I had been searching for.

Although the details of a situation aren't as important as how
the experience made one feel, I attempt to share both with you
within these pages. Living life, I have learned that emotions are
the oars that maneuver the boat to turn us in directions down the
river of life we might not have chosen otherwise. Sometimes rowing
upstream, against the current, another time taking a tributary along
the way that branches into a new direction only to find ourselves

lost, we are still determined to make our own way, yet we miss all the beauty in our headstrong determination. Tired, exhausted, discouraged, and weary, we finally come to the day when we accept that we are lost and simply rest our oars, allowing the river to take us where it will—only to arrive where we were always meant to be.

Instead of waiting until the end of life for a "life review," I made the choice to begin one midstream, while there was still time to change course. Turning myself back into myself, I was about to find myself and to change my story so I could write a new one. With this, the life review began.

Chapter 1

SORRY FOR YOUR LUCK—HERE I AM!

A weed is no more than a flower in disguise.

—James Russell Lowe

*O*nce upon a time, there lived a couple in their late thirties. Having struggled through the Great Depression, extreme poverty, and the loss of their dreams, they found that life was finally pretty good. The man had a good job, making good wages. Their two older children were independent. And the woman was ready for a life of freedom at a job she enjoyed after caring for others her whole life. Their life was full of friends, weekends camping or out dancing, and many gatherings for cards and socializing. One day while at work, the woman passed out. Coming to, she knew she was pregnant, and with this realization, fear shot through her mind at all the changes about to come her way. Inwardly, she screamed, *No!* Her life flashed before her. She saw her newfound freedom gone, the rejection of friends who had no young children to care for, and the return to the daily life of caring for others' needs and never her own. Her fear soon evolved to resentment when she heard her husband tell his friends, "I'd rather she was home pregnant than out working."

Finally, on a snowy, cold day, a little girl was born. The labor had been long, hard, and painful, a story that would often be told and retold to the little girl growing up. There was no celebration, only a sullen acceptance.

While the woman returned home to care once again for others, her husband continued working and enjoying his friends. As his friends began to buy cabins in the northern woods, he soon jumped on board, and a small cabin was purchased. The woman was relegated to packing for five, purchasing food she would cook the whole weekend, and caring for her new baby. After many hours of travel, the others would run out to fish, swim, and explore, while she remained behind to clean, cook, and tend to a baby's needs. At the end of the weekend, she would pack and clean, only to return home to cook and clean all week and then to face the weekend once again. There was no end in sight, and resentment was allowed to grow, beginning to obscure all else in her life.

The little girl's older siblings had full lives, finally leaving for college and the military, so the woman was left alone with the little girl … and the man. By the time the older children returned, the parents and the life they remembered growing up was gone. All the friends had disappeared, as the woman feared rejection due to her new status as a mother with a young child and had declined their invitations to join them for weekend activities of fun and enjoyment. The pleasure the man and woman had enjoyed was gone, replaced by resentment smoldering into bitterness, and a wall of division was growing between them. The little girl knew none of this, being raised in the only environment she knew, but it was seen by those observing.

This is written in the third person, as an outsider looking in, as I remember none of this, only what I have been told by my family and those around me who knew them well. My own first memories were at age three, standing on the couch next to my mother as she read the daily newspaper and pointing at words, wanting to know what they meant, what they said, how they were put together to mean something. I was fascinated with these symbols on paper and wanted to know. My mother's dream when young was to be a teacher, so she was patient with me, teaching what I wanted to know. And at age three, I could read. Seeing this, my mother began buying me books to occupy my time. They became my treasures, my whole world, and I would lose myself in these amazing letters that became meaningful words. They opened up new realms for me to explore and discover.

It was a true gift that I'd found reading, as I was often alone. My mother had her weekly schedule, which she adhered to religiously. I always knew what day of the week it was by what she was doing that day. Left to find my own entertainment, I grew to love the silence and being alone with my books and my imagination. Often, I would make a small fort out of cushions and a blanket. I had my own little world where imaginary friends came to play and share in my adventures. Having many, I vividly remember our hours of conversation, talking, and laughing in our own little world until, after a while, they would leave. Then I would grab my books and go on journeys to foreign lands I longed to see with people I longed to meet. As my books were children's stories, I met gypsies, fairies, mermaids, witches, talking animals, and women with flowing hair and radiant beauty. It was a wonderful world, where I could shape-shift my reality into whatever and whoever I wanted to be. I was free to choose, so I was never bored. Eventually, my mother bought me paper and colored pencils, and I would record my own adventures, tales of exotic beings and travels into the unknown. My imagination was rich, and so was my life.

Although I was bought dolls of various shapes and sizes, I preferred my own world to any of them. So leaving them piled in a corner, I would find my cat and sing songs I would make up as I went along. He tolerated me well. Hearing me sing, my mother began buying me albums. There were two that I remember playing over and over again. One was all the songs of the United States military, which I learned by heart. The words were empowering and soulful, filled with loyalty, and centered on caring for and protecting others. The other album was by the Singing Nuns. Every song was in Latin, but the album cover had the words in English. I quickly learned these songs, as they touched me deep inside. As I sang, I would sometimes cry, feeling such a sense of peace and love that I would later seek to find in a hundred different ways, leading me into a hundred different experiences until I found the source at last. That discovery was to be a long time coming.

Seeing my love of music, my mother decided it was time for me to learn how to play the piano. She was a very accomplished pianist, who would often sit and play in the afternoons while dad was at work. This was time for just the two of us, and she would play and teach me the words to the songs—happy, playful songs and beautiful hymns she played often in church. With a love for words, I learned all the songs quickly, and this was a happy time.

Then she decided it was my turn to sit at the piano and begin to learn to play for myself. This was totally foreign for me, having fingers that forgot their role, while reading symbols on a piece of paper that I did not understand—not words but strange shapes I was expected to make sense of. And I was left alone again. My mother was determined I would follow her passion. My older siblings had both failed, so I was her last hope. Forced to sit alone at the piano for one to two hours a day to practice, I would often end up just sitting there crying. This was torture. And although I did try to make sense of it all, after two years and, to my great relief, she finally gave up. Her disappointment was strong, and she let it be known. When she was upset, she would get out the sweeper and sweep until I thought the carpet would be sucked up, so I learned quickly to get out of her way, sensing that I, too, might be swept up and out of her sight. To this day, the sound of a sweeper sets me on edge.

My mother belonged to a small local church, where she was the pianist and where I attended Sunday school every Sunday morning. I loved Sunday school! Books, words, and stories of people I had never met and adventures I had never heard before but longed to live. Learning them all, I could tell them as well as the Sunday school teacher. This led my mother to buy me a volume of children's Bible stories, and I devoured them. While I enjoyed learning, these stories confused and terrified me, as I read about somebody called God kicking his own kids out of their home because they ate an apple; killing thousands of people and animals in a flood because he got mad at them; nailing some guy to a tree just because he was a good person everybody liked; and, on top of all that, being determined to send all of us to this lake of fire where we would burn forever and ever. These stories filled me with fear, and my questions in Sunday school were met with vague answers that never explained to me why so many people had to suffer and die, except that this was someone named God's punishment. But for what, I didn't understand. Fear drove me away from this "God" everyone seemed to want me to get to know and accept as mine, but the questions would remain embedded in my mind until I later found answers.

Little time was spent with my father, a carpenter by trade. Because I was a girl, he had little interest in teaching me his trade, but I wanted to spend more time with him, so I asked to learn. He gave me scraps of wood, a few nails, and a hammer and told me to build a birdhouse. Hours later, when I showed him a mangled mess of wood and nails, he said nothing. But my carpentry days were over, and I went back to my books and solitude.

As time went on, in the summer, I would play with our cats and dogs outside. And the few neighborhood kids would come around to play tag, make mud pies in the dirt road, or do whatever else our imaginations could think of. Summers also brought the weekend trips back and forth to the cabin, and I was allowed to take a friend with me. As I had a fear of water, instilled in me by my mother who couldn't swim, while my friends would splash and swim, I would be busy catching crawfish to examine and talk to. I would ask them what they ate or if they had any family around before putting them safely out of the way of my friends' feet. Life was pretty good, as it was all I knew.

Through the experiences of what seems like a hundred years, I now see life in a new way. We arrive in this realm free and radiant light, ready for an adventure, to explore, discover, and smell all the roses we find around us. Then we are handed our welcome gift as those around us say, "Here, you get all my thoughts and fears, my judgments and beliefs, along with the inheritance of traditions of your great-great-great-grandparents—you get it *all!*" It's a big, heavy burden we get to carry for the rest of our life, dimming our light and robbing us of our freedom, starting at a young age. We are still here, somewhere, buried under this heavy burden.

The stories I was to hear growing up about my new life were the stories of a weed that had suddenly appeared and would grow and strangle the crop of my parents' life, not a flower to enhance their life together. These stories were all based on the thoughts, fears, and judgments of those around me. But how was I to know? As I listened and believed them, these stories would begin to paint a picture of who I was and would later view myself to be. It wasn't a very pretty picture.

But not knowing that then, I needed to see it now, for I was seeking the truth about myself.

It was like watching a movie. I began to see that my mother's bitter, resentful thoughts would be the weed that was allowed to grow and strangle what my parents once had. It wasn't me at all, but her own chosen thoughts. This was a truth that flooded me with great relief.

In the next scene, I viewed a happy child, ignorant of what was occurring around her, using her very vivid imagination by living for the moment and creating a world that was bright and fun and full of adventures, travels, and friends. As she grew, this imagination would turn against her, as she began to form a whole new vivid image of herself. It was here that I began to lose who I am.

Viewing this small portion of my life, now recognizing it was not me that ruined my parents' life, I could understand that my parents loved me the best they could with the limited knowledge they had. Simply following the patterns handed to them by their own parents, they would raise me as they had been raised without ever really looking at this child as an individual but with the expectation that I would be like them, as they had become like their own parents. They were to be very surprised in the days to come, but that is a story for later. For now, seeing the truth of what had occurred, I was given a gift, the gift of self-forgiveness, as I had done nothing wrong.

There was one more gift I was to receive in looking back. And that is where my perception of marriage came from. Living within a marriage that was dissolving, I never heard honest communication or laughter, never saw intimacy or love, but lived in brewing resentment and the concept that marriage and children were a burden to be endured as a woman. Given that I would base my own future marriages on what I had learned, it came as no surprise that they failed. Oh, I was learning all right and thankful for it.

With a new understanding gained, it is with a tinge of sadness for all of us that I move into the next chapter to find what else I must discover on my journey to find out who I am.

Chapter 2

JUST A CHILD ... WITH A VOICE
NO ONE WANTED TO HEAR

Nobody knows I'm there, yet I know everything.

—Anna Paszkiewicz

*A*t this time of my life, my education about life beyond my narrow borders of innocence and ignorance began. It was a time I was about to replace my thoughts for others and lose who I came here to be. My life was about to make a dramatic change.

When I was around age four or five, my sister would occasionally stay at our house when she was home on school break. And when our mother would go shopping or run errands, my sister would watch me. Having been a picky eater from birth, I would spit out foods I didn't like and refuse to eat until something filled my mouth that I liked. My mother had adapted to my taste in food, sometimes making separate meals apart from what she and my father would eat just so that I would eat. My sister hadn't been around much since I was two years old and heated up a potpie one day for my lunch, not realizing that I hated potpies and was never forced to eat one.

As I sat at the table and refused to put one bite in my mouth, she became furious! A floodgate of anger opened, and she began to literally scream that I was too much work, not worth the effort her mother was making to cater to me, and it was no wonder that their life was so messed up! On a roll, she accused me of ruining her parents' marriage, adding that I was nothing but a burden and that she wished I had never been born.

Staring at her, I remember thinking that I just didn't want to eat that potpie! But I also heard the words "burden," "your fault," and "not worth it" and the message that I had "destroyed everything" by being here. There was no way I could know then the effect my presence was having on those around me or how my parents' marriage had disintegrated, as I knew no other life than the one I had been living and experiencing. In that explosion, I first learned that things were not as they appeared, and somehow I was all to blame.

From then on, I began watching my parents. Every time they were angry, I felt that it somehow had to be at something I had said or done. So I learned to be on guard and observe their actions, trying to make sure that I didn't get in their way and be a burden.

As time went on, my sister began to tell me stories about the wonderful life she had grown up in. She shared stories about camping, big groups playing cards, and dancing every weekend with lots of friends and a lot of fun and about the great life they had together—always adding, "Until you came along." This was totally different than the life I was living. My parents rarely went anywhere, had no friends, and never did anything fun. If this was all true, and it must be if she said it, then I really had ruined everything by showing up. Lying in bed at night, I would wish that I could have been with them back then, having all that fun she talked about and wondering what I had done to change everything so much. Alone with my thoughts, I began to withdraw, pulling further and further into myself and thinking about all the damage I had caused, even though I didn't understand why, as I was just a little girl.

After this, being alone became my sanctuary. "Out there" I seemed to be causing a whole lot of problems. Within this sanctuary, I learned to listen, as clearly, from what I'd been told, life was not as it appeared to be and there was much more I needed to learn. Listening, I learned much, both from what was said, as well as what was unsaid from those around me. Watching faces and body language, I quickly understood that what was being said was not always what was truly meant. Everywhere we went, I watched and listened.

In an effort to fit in and join with conversations, I began to innocently share what I was learning from those around me. Not only did I share what I was intuitively picking up from conversations in the home, I shared things that I saw in other people when we were out at family gatherings. My mother was appalled and then angry, and I learned quickly that what I knew was *not* appreciated.

Instead of talking about it, she would yell, adding that good girls were to be seen and not heard. So I would run away to be alone and cry, not understanding exactly what I had done to be punished for, but learning it was much safer to keep my knowing to myself and my mouth shut. It truly was better, and much safer, to be seen and not heard.

Soon after, another lesson learned was not to say the words "I know" when something was said to me. These words aggravated my sister, who began to disgustedly call me a "know-it-all." And I again learned to keep quiet. But, in truth, I *did* know! My gifts of listening and observing taught me much, and I could have shared many things with others that they did not know, if anyone had taken the time to listen. But no one wanted to hear this small voice that seemed to know too much. And I learned to silence it, withdrawing even further and simply listening, alone with my knowing.

At age five, it was time to enter school. I remember standing there sobbing outside the door with my mother, as I didn't want to leave the world I had created at home. What I was seeing was unlike anything I had ever encountered—kids, kids, and more kids

I did not know, with no clue how to interact with them. This was a scary world, as I had developed no real social skills, interacting seldom with others outside my family and learning that the less I said, the better off I would be.

Over time, I settled in, discovering new books, new words, and new adventures to explore in learning. And because I already knew the basics of counting, reading, and tying my shoes, I was left to read whatever I could find in this wonderful world that held so many books. Being away from home wasn't all that bad.

Flourishing in school and always at the top of my class, my teachers loved me. I was always "teacher's pet," often asked to tutor other students who were struggling in their learning. At recess, I chose to hang out with my teachers, as I was more accustomed to the company of adults than that of kids, and they would talk while I listened. Being a good listener, as I now knew it was not safe to speak, I was unknowingly drawing information out of others. My teachers shared a lot with me about their families, their lives, and what they believed. Beginning to feel safe in their acceptance, I began to share my life at home, telling them all about my family; and they began to learn a lot as well.

At parent-teacher conferences, my mother was shocked at what my teachers knew. And once she was home, I would be firmly told to keep quiet and never to share what was going on at home! So, no voice at home and now no voice at school, which had been my only outlet to share at the time. I again kept my thoughts to myself, understanding that never, under any circumstances, was I to speak or be myself, as to be myself was to be criticized, judged, and punished. I heard again the message that it was much better to be seen and not heard. To be a "good girl" was to be a silent girl and to never stand out, or you became a target for others. And although I still had a lot of thoughts, no one cared to listen, and no one ever asked. In my little silent world, alone with my thoughts, I began a long lifetime of keeping my voice silenced. It was better to be quiet and listen than to speak and draw reproach. And I had learned this lesson well. Donning the mask of silent, obedient child, I learned this served me well at the time, and I began to disappear.

There was so much that was buried here that I had never seen before. With each new sight came a greater awareness of both myself and others. It was through ignorance that I believed the pain, anger, and frustration I was feeling from others was all caused by me and that, somehow, it was all my fault because I was in the way, a burden and unworthy of love or acceptance from others. It was here that the self-image I would carry with me was being formed to influence and direct my life.

It was here that I became aware that I was different than my family, and this difference frightened them. In their fear, I would begin to hear, *How dare you be different, think differently, see differently than what I see? How dare you be yourself?!* In an attempt to control what they feared, guilt became the tool used to tether this totally unknown child from being free. It was here that I began to lose sight of my true self. It was painful for me to see.

Yet, truth can be found in the midst of pain, the richest of truths being understanding and forgiveness, for it was here that I began to understand and forgive my sister. Reacting out of her own pain at the demise of our parents' relationship, one she idolized and had set as her own goal to achieve, she had looked around for what had changed. All she saw was me, and I was blamed. She had no idea of the harm she was causing or of the image her words were causing me to see. And I could finally let it go, setting both of us free.

There was more to see. When we are born, we know who we are. As thoughts are instilled within us from without, we begin to see only these thoughts and lose our identity, seeing all things through the thoughts given to us. This is called living blind, and this was how I had lived. It was becoming so clear to me now in looking back that, as a little one, I was fulfilling my purpose for being here.

My purpose is to see, to know, and to share what I saw and knew. Although this purpose was discouraged, called bad, and I was told to silence myself, it was in seeing this now I realized that this imposed silence had actually been my training ground, where I would learn how to listen within. This new insight instilled a determination to walk free in the purpose that I had come here to fulfill. Seeing is an essential part of knowing, as when the truth is unseen, it is unknown and an error in thought cannot be corrected. In seeing, I know that correction is taking place, and I will one day be healed and whole and ready to take up my purpose once again. It was others' fears that put me in this prison of silence. But, although a part of my mind was imprisoned there, my heart has continued to prepare for the day my voice would be set free. When it is, I am sure I will find that it has grown rich and sweet with the passing of time, like a fine wine ready to be poured forth.

Was this review worth the pain I experienced? More than words can convey, as lies had been ripped away to reveal the truth. Feeling freer for finally seeing, I am ready to continue forward into what is ahead.

Chapter 3

LOST IN LABEL LAND: WHO AM I?!

What's in a name? That which we call a rose
by any other name would smell as sweet.

—William Shakespeare

Our world is a jumbled-up mass of words applied as names and labels and then given meaning by those around us. We have assigned a label to everything from a blade of grass and a flower and a chair to ourselves and the divine and everything in between, all in an attempt to understand. We spread labels around like seeds to grow and produce with no thought as to whether we are planting weeds or beauty to bloom. Labels begin at birth, when we are given a name we did not choose but will be known by for the rest of our life. This is just the beginning, as we are in a land of labels that fly like dust around us, seeking someplace to land. The key is not to get lost in Label Land and lose our way. Yet, when we are young and clueless, getting lost is easy to do.

By now, I was becoming confident enough in school to begin making friends, a handful of kids who I seemed drawn to and was comfortable being around. During recess, we would play our own games, usually involving some kind of fantasy we would act out, just having fun. But when it rained, I was on a mission. Worms would crawl up from the grass surrounding the cement playground and I knew that their lives were in jeopardy if I did not pick up and rescue each and every one. By the handfuls, I would carry them back into the grassy areas and drop them off where they would be safe. My new friends accepted this. Some would help, while others, those more squeamish, would wait until our rescue mission was accomplished. With friends around me who let me be me and accepted me, I was happy!

At the same time, kids were moving into my neighborhood. With my confidence building at school, I quickly became friends with everyone and eventually, unknowingly, moved into the role of leader of the neighborhood. After school and on the weekends, they would wait for me to decide what we would do that day. And I would lead them to new discoveries in the nearby woods and pond or on bike rides or in a fun game of softball or kickball. There was always something to do. Life was pretty good and just seemed to be getting better.

In expanding my boundaries, meeting new people at home and at school, I was opening the door to a new experience into the land of labels, an experience that would again change how I viewed myself. Unknowingly, I was walking into a foreign land full of lions, tigers, and bears, oh my, with no known tools available to protect myself.

As I moved through school, the personalities around me began to change as children adapted to what they were being taught at home and brought their lessons to school. Not all of it was good or kind. With a long narrow face and close-cropped hair, hair kept very short, as it was easier to maintain; ears that I had not yet grown into; and large protruding teeth, I soon became a target. First, I was given the label Dumbo the Elephant, followed by Bucky Beaver. While some would laugh, I did not, as their labels were affecting how I saw myself, and the picture was very ugly.

15

Toward the end of grade school, I was given another label that would attempt to rob me of the joy I found in learning. At that time, we were tested at school and, with my extremely high scores, my mother was told her daughter was a genius. I had no clue what this meant. My mother, though, became obsessed with this label, and her expectations became high. The pressure to excel was intense, as straight A's were now expected, never rewarded, and anything less demanded an answer. Coming to hate this label, I would later run from it.

Many labels were flying my way at a very young age, compressing me into an image of the labels I was hearing, but there was another label coming that would change the trajectory of my life for many years.

There was a birthday party for one of my friends in the neighborhood, and everyone was invited, including an older boy who was often left out of our fun. This was through no fault of our own, but because he viewed himself as older and better than us younger kids and refused to join us. Halfway through our fun party, he asked if we wanted to play a game. Sure, we all yelled, as what child doesn't love a game?! His game was to go around the table and give each of us a label based on who he saw us as being. As he went around the table, giving each of us a label, we would smile and laugh; the labels were funny and cute. Then my turn came, and although I did not know it, this boy did not like me. He was jealous and envious that I was leader in the neighborhood, feeling that he should be, as he was older than me. With a sneer on his face, he announced my label as "the bossy cow," adding, "because you're a know-it-all and are always telling others what to do." The moment still stands out vividly, as this label hit me like an arrow into my very heart. The buried memories of being shunned and silenced for being a know-it-all rushed back, and with those memories, came the pain of rejection and the fear of being noticed for standing out. I froze.

My face must have reflected the pain I was feeling, as everyone at the table grew silent watching me, except for the older boy, who proceeded to laugh, knowing he had hit the target he was aiming for. Standing up from the table with tears in my eyes, I went home, a wounded, fallen leader. This label was to change my life for many years, as my very strength, the leader I had grown to be, had been attacked and my newfound self-confidence was not yet developed enough to maintain. This was too much like a repeat of the past, and I would again begin to fade into nonexistence. Vowing inwardly to never again stand out, I would withdraw once and for all and not be heard or seen, believing the pain was too great.

This began my years of following others. One day, I made a new friend at school. To me, she was beautiful, everything I had ever wanted to be, with beautiful hair, bright light eyes, and shapely beyond her young years. I began to idolize her. Her mother was young and bought her pretty, expensive clothes, took her to a professional hairstylist, and allowed her to wear makeup. We became close friends, doing everything together. And I began to beg my older, very conservative mother to let me style my hair differently, to wear makeup, to pierce my ears, and to buy store-bought clothes instead of wearing the handmade clothes she had always made for me.

She slowly relented to one plea at a time, as I began to form myself into my friend's image. By then, I had buried my own identity and made the choice to copy hers. Yet all these outer changes were never enough to change how I saw myself inside, and I began to apply labels to myself, comparing myself to my new friend. They were ugly labels, as I identified my every imagined deficit in comparing myself to her, never seeing myself for who I was. An aversion to mirrors started here, and I would turn my head when I would walk by, not wanting to see this very ugly, lacking girl. Not recognizing the slow disintegration of who I came here to be, I no longer knew who I was, for I was lost in Label Land.

Word upon word, label upon label, my self-worth was paying the price. My thoughts were based upon the words I had heard, thoughts molding and shaping an image of myself to lead me through life. This would endure until I heard other words, words that changed the thoughts I held about myself, thereby changing the image that I saw as myself. Sticks and stones may break my bones, but labels were surely killing me at the time, killing the me that I came here to be.

Years later, while looking at old pictures from the past, I could hardly believe how beautiful I was as a teenager and young woman. Nor could I believe I never saw it! My whole perception of myself was based on childhood—on shorn hair, buck teeth, big ears, and labels—so that every time I looked in the mirror, it was not me that I saw, but this ugly, worthless person of no value, no beauty, and nothing to offer anyone. It was hard to believe as I stared at these pictures. But doing so showed me much about perception and illusion and how powerful our thoughts about ourselves are to influence who we see, how we live, and who we present ourselves to be—a lie based on thoughts planted by the words we hear.

None of us are alone in this Land of Labels. Labels are too often used to suppress and categorize and put each other in nice, neat little boxes, where we will remain unseen and unheard, believing this is where we belong. Feeling the pain of being lost, I had to ask myself, Where, exactly, do I want to belong? Do I want to be like everyone else, forsaking my true, individual, unique identity for fear of being labeled an outcast?

It was in asking these questions that I first began to discover my one true self, long buried under all these labels, but patiently waiting to be found. My heart was determined to find me, but I had a lot of unburying to do before I could find this self that is who I am. In my attempt to protect myself long ago, I had withdrawn into a dark cocoon. And while that cocoon was warm and seemingly secure, I had actually wrapped myself in a self-made prison. In the dark, I heard nothing but an echo of the words that had been spoken to me, forming a false perception of who I was and holding me back from being. In this prison I would stay until, in later years, this cocoon became old, tattered, and worn, and the light began to shine in so that I could truly see my true self. I was not a lowly worm, unworthy of love but a butterfly being formed to finally, one day, emerge and fly free. It was in finally asking myself who I wanted to be that I felt a stirring in this dark cocoon, and I knew I was on my way to finding out the truth about who I am.

While in many ways, this review was painful, it seemed to be a pain that was cracking open my heart, allowing compassion and understanding to flow in and influence my every thought. It was with a sense of freedom that I could look at the harm labels had done to me and see the harm they are doing to others. No longer could I assign a label to another to imprison him or her as I had been imprisoned. It was the beginning of searching for truth, as I began to truly look at others, determined to see below the label and find the real person who stood before me. Every time, I found great beauty within him or her—a beauty just waiting to be seen, recognized, accepted, and loved.

Feeling the pain being slowly transformed into excitement, I knew this was a breakthrough in finding the me I had lost. It was with new eyes that I was ready to venture forth into yet another chapter of life and clearly see what I had missed before.

Chapter 4

STUCK IN THE MIDDLE WITH YOU: THIS SUCKS!

You have brains in your head. You have
feet in your shoes. You can steer yourself
in any direction you choose.

—Dr. Seuss

Nearing high school, my world began to shift and change. And not pleasantly. My friend since grade school developed a new friendship. It had always been just the two of us for many years, and I was terrified. While I had a few other neighborhood friends, I was close to no one else but her. In desperation, I wrote her a long letter, explaining my love and devotion and how it hurt me to see her turn toward another. In trembling anticipation, I waited for her response. In my heart, I wanted her reassurance, her pledge of unending friendship, and for her to again turn to me as her one and only true friend. This was not to be. Later, she walked by me in the hallway with her new friend and, with a smirk on her face, told me,

"Yes, I've read it," and kept on walking. With my heart breaking, I stood alone in the hallway in tears.

Like a robot, I went through my classes in a daze, day after day, doing what I was supposed to do, how I was supposed to do it and eventually resigned myself to my new state of being alone again. As in the past, I turned to reading and, later, writing, which seemed to ease my pain. But my mother found my diary, read it, and became angry, as I also wrote about what was happening at home. This was the end of writing for a while. So, I just waited alone for time to pass.

At home, my parents' relationship had hit an all-time low. The kiss before my father left for work had long before disappeared and there was no hello at the end of the day when he returned. I watched. At the dinner table, we either ate in silence, or my mother would begin her tirade about who and what I should be. As this continued night after night, my father finally erupted in seldom seen anger and he would tell her to *stop!* Mom's continual verbal beating on me was the only thing he responded to, the only time he acknowledged me. And I knew then that he had been experiencing the same criticism directed at him for many years. After dinner, my dad would go into the living room and read his paper while I helped my mom clean up after dinner. The silence was thick and the strain enormous!

One morning, I woke up to yelling. My parents never yelled, rarely ever talked, so I listened with an anxious feeling inside as I heard dad yell, "When she is out of school, I am leaving here." Hearing this, I lay there stiff and silent, thinking about their unhappiness and how, again, I must be to blame.

This began a thirteen-month period where my parents did not speak to one another. To communicate, my parents used me as their go-between. Mom would give me a message to take to my dad, who spent most of his time on the weekends in the garage tinkering with tools and projects to stay out of the house and away from mom. Simply sharing mom's message, I would return to her with an answer. It was usually not the one she wanted, and she would begin to berate and criticize dad to me. She shared her frustration and resentment, going far back into the past. And I heard things I did not want to hear and should never have heard. Yet I listened quietly, not daring say a word for fear this anger and resentment would be turned on me.

As time went on, my dad began to do the same thing when I would visit him with a message. More stories of the past would erupt like a volcano, really not mine to hear but influencing me just the same. I felt like a stranger in a very strange land.

There were times dad would disappear, and we would later discover he had walked the mile and a half to my sister's home and would sit and pour out his pain, his frustration, and his plans to leave once I was out of school. This thought filled me with dread, as I had another three years to go before graduating! Not wanting to live another three years ensnared in this painful nest of turmoil, I began to wish he would leave now. And maybe, just maybe, one of them would be happy, and I could live with the happy one. My wish was not to be.

When my mother discovered what he had been doing, she began to take me over to my sister's home. There she would pour out her own anger and resentment, her side of the story, while I sat and listened. My sister now saw that there was more going on at home than she had ever known, and her attitude toward me began to soften. Seeing that I was stuck in the middle, she was concerned. But by that time, I held no trust for her and/or her concern for my well-being. Instead of making time for me, allowing me to share all the fear and turmoil boiling inside of me, she began instead to buy me extravagant and costly gifts. Stubbornly, I made it a point to show that I disliked them all and refused to acknowledge her gestures to reconcile. Having learned from example, I was choosing to live within my own world of anger, resentment, and blame.

At home, I was living within boiling, unspoken anger with heavy silence all around me. Nearing the end of junior high, my mother became sick—very sick. She had had pneumonia for many months, telling no one and refusing treatment. When the pain became too much, she finally went to the doctor, who put her in the hospital immediately. She had allowed the sickness to continue so long that it had destroyed a large portion of her lungs, and she was ordered to stay in the hospital for two weeks, undergoing extensive treatments. My father assumed the role of making sure I was up and ready for school and taking me to my graduation to receive my certificate.

Life seemed much more peaceful during this time. In the evenings and the weekend, dad would take me to see my mother in the hospital. At first, he would wait in the car for me to return, but he eventually began to come into mom's room with me. After a few days, they began to make small talk, the first words spoken to each other in thirteen months. After a few such visits, I began to leave the room, allowing them time to talk alone.

I never knew what they talked about, but when my mother finally left the hospital, they were at least talking, and the silence had ended. Their relationship was never the same again. But as they were now speaking to each other, my time as go-between had come to an end. Still, the damage had already occurred, influencing once more my thoughts about myself, about marriage, and about both of them, and nothing would ever be the same.

During those thirteen months, my mother had begun to depend on me for her emotional support. And even after she and my dad began to talk again, she continued to share her feelings and her resentments of years long past and to look to me as confidante. This was a one-sided relationship, as I never shared my feelings, my struggles, and my thoughts, and she never asked. Mine was still a voice no one wanted to hear. Throughout the summer, her dependency continued to grow, and this itself was a heavy burden to carry. It was at this time that thoughts of running began to circulate through my mind. To get away from all this resentment and dependency that was sucking me into such a dark place, I longed for freedom, for friends that I could talk with and share with and an outlet for my own fear, anger, and resentment.

Entering high school, I found it such a relief to get away from home. New classes, new faces, and new experiences were all around me. Then the pressure began to select a college prep curriculum. With that came the question, "What do you want to be when you grow up?" Ensured a full ride to any college or university, I was told it was time to decide and decide now.

When my mother asked, I told her that my deepest desire was to be a model. To be free, to travel, and to dress in beautiful clothes with professional artists fixing my hair and designing my face into one of beauty was what I had been dreaming about.

"You *what?!*" is the response I received.

This desire was quickly dismissed as being too insecure, too risky, and unstable, with no steady, reliable source of income and chances of failure high. My mother's plan for me was to find a good job, marry, have children and be "normal." The thought of getting a secure job; marrying; having children; and being bound to the constant needs of others, cooking, cleaning, working, and providing for those around me—with every ounce of energy focused outward instead of inward to my heart's desires—sounded like literal prison to me! Oh no! Not me! My mind was already made up, and I would rebel against following this path for the rest of my life, as I knew it wasn't me or who I wanted to be.

As being a model was the only answer I had, the only desire in my heart at the time, I left the decision for my future to my mother, and she proceeded to enroll me in the secretarial curriculum. She explained that a good secretary would always have a job and would always be needed, and I would always be independent in earning my own source of income. "Whatever," was my reply.

Unknowingly, I had taken a step in the footprints of my mother. Her dream, her deepest desire when she was young was to be a teacher. But her mother, like mine, had told her the goal she had for herself was too insecure and not safe and she was to choose the safety and security of being a wife and mother. Did my mother know this? There is no doubt she did not; nor did I at the time. She was just leading me to follow in her footsteps, footsteps she had been led on by her own mother, leaving her full of resentment. So, I begin my first year of high school with resentment and no true enthusiasm, other than to be somewhere other than home.

Still leery of forming close friendships, I pretty much kept to myself at school. But I was in an environment wherein I excelled and made my straight A's, soon becoming a favorite among my teachers. It was not enough, and I hungered to belong and not just for a few hours a day. Around me, I was experiencing a whole new world, seeing a mishmash of different clothing, lifestyles, and ways that I had never seen or heard. This was the hippy era, and the more I watched, the more this appealed to me, as it reminded me of the gypsy I had once imagined myself to be. Living a life of exotic dress, freedom to roam, and a total disregard for the norms of society was very appealing. While I continued to excel in school, school became secondary, as I continued to observe the lives of those around me.

Midway through the year, I found myself sitting next to two very interesting girls my age in class. They were both like no one I had ever met before. Both appeared very confident, self-assured, and worldly-wise, and I was fascinated just listening to them. Telling stories of sexual escapades, hitchhiking to new and exciting places, and experimenting with drugs, they introduced me to a world that was very new, very exciting, and very appealing. Inwardly searching for freedom, I was drawn like a moth to a flame. We soon became friends, and I was about to embark on a wild, amazing adventure into the unknown.

Freedom begins in the mind and listening to the innate desires the heart holds. Yet a mind filled with turmoil and guilt was no environment to formulate a successful plan for the freedom I sought. Led by my desire to escape, I was to begin a search for this elusive freedom in the months to come. Yes, I had a brain, a brain filled with chaos. And I had the feet, feet ready to run. And Dr. Seuss was right, as I was about to steer myself in the direction I was to choose.

To know then what I know now, I ask myself, *Would I have chosen differently?* I think not. It was part of the journey of experience, from which I would emerge singed and burned but knowing more now than I knew then. This knowledge would one day be of great value. With a sense of excitement and courage, I was about to follow my heart and step onto the wild ride called the roller coaster of life!

Chapter 5

THE ROAD TO FREEDOM?
MAYBE ... MAYBE NOT!

Everything I did in my life that was
worthwhile, I caught hell for.

—Earl Warren

My mother still held the reins of control, and she wondered about my new friends, insisting on meeting their parents before allowing me to spend time with them. As they appeared presentable, I was given the green light to stay overnight at their homes. She was clueless as to what would occur, as she had no idea such wild, crazy times existed. She was also unaware that my friends' parents were often out of town and gone for the night, allowing their daughters freedom to roam. My mother was still expecting me to be like my older sister and adhere to the rules set before me, trusting that I would become who she had chosen me to be. She didn't know me, had never made any attempt to know me, and I felt free to explore this new realm I had found.

With my new friends, I began to explore this unfamiliar but

very appealing world they lived in. Spending nights with one or both of them, I experienced my first drunk and my first taste of the adventures to be had on hallucinogens. Here, I was introduced to the freedom of hitchhiking as we hitched rides through town and into other nearby cities to see the sights and meet new people. We had wild, crazy, and exciting times, unlike anything I had ever known. This was indeed a whole new world, and I was enjoying myself!

There was so much to learn. In our long drug-filled nights and in conversations during the day at school, my friends began to regal me with stories of all their sexual exploits. Both had begun quite young and had much to tell. They informed me I was much too old to be a virgin and, at age sixteen, it was time to "get over it" and experience it for myself. Although sex held no appeal for me, the pressure was on to conform to this new way of life with my new friends. I didn't see that I was simply trading one set of rules for another.

Joining with some neighborhood friends one night, high on whatever drug was available and drinking anything at hand, I made the decision that tonight was the night. Looking around me, I tried to decide which boy to choose. None attracted me, but they were all available and ready to take advantage of the opportunity being offered, so I made my decision. There, in a dirty bedroom, I experienced sex. Painful, the moment held no special meaning for me; I did my duty, and bleeding and in pain, I went home. The next day at school, I proudly announced to my friends that I was no longer a virgin. High fives all around, with hugs and congratulations; I had my reward for the sacrifice made.

This began a cycle of reoccurring sexual experiences with different guys, picked up here and there when I was out with my friends. There was no end to the opportunities presented. Sex still held no appeal for me, no pleasure or satisfaction, but I learned to enjoy the challenge of conquering. It became a game, a game where I added notches to my belt, more than I can recall. Now one with my friends, I continued to follow in their footsteps. Their footsteps quickly led me into a downward spiraling world of experiences that soon overcame me. And it wasn't long before I began skipping school, hitchhiking throughout town, picking up boys to later discard, and following whatever new adventure I could find.

My mother began to sense the change in me, and our relationship began to change as well. She realized she did not have the control over me she thought she had and was faced with the decision to either fight this new lifestyle or acquiesce and hope for the best. She relented and allowed me my freedom. But this freedom came with a price, as relentless verbal tirades began, for her fear turned to anger and bitter resentment. It was at this time that I earned the label *rebel*. For her, I had lost my given name and would be known in her mind as rebel for the rest of her life. Feeling my own resentment, I chose to wear this new label proudly, although, in my heart, the word hurt; I felt that it labeled me as an outcast in my family, still not really belonging, because I was, again, the first to step outside their box.

With the atmosphere at home and the new lifestyle I was now submerged in, I spent more and more time away, beginning to skip school two or three days a week. It was easy to maintain my straight A school average, as school was always easy. My absence was not missed or reported, for I was still excelling in all my classes.

In my days of freedom from school and home, I slowly wandered away from my two friends, as I was meeting new people everywhere I went. Soon, I was introduced to some people who had their own place in town. All kids my age, sixteen to twenty, they appeared to me to be living the life. Outcasts from their own families, they had formed their own, and I fit right in. Soon, I was spending many hours there.

By now, school had lost any meaning. What, really, did I have to work toward or look forward to? A life as a secretary, working forty hours a week at a job with no meaning, other than to provide an income and wait for the years to pass until I could retire with a pension? This was a path someone else had chosen for me and one I did not care to travel. While I wasn't sure what it was I wanted, I knew for sure what I did not want.

One day, in the middle of the eleventh grade, I quit school. And there was nothing my mother could do; I just refused to attend. She begged me to at least attend an alternative school, so that I would someday graduate, and I finally agreed. Instead of a bus taking me to and from school, she would have to drive me across town to attend. On the way there every morning, she would rant and rave about what a disappointment I was, how rebellious I was being, and how much work I was causing her.

One morning, she told me she wished I'd never been born and that I wasn't living in her home. Choosing this as my escape, instead of going home after school that day, I moved in with my new friends and called her to inform her I was not returning. She begged me to come home, but I reminded her of what she had said and hung up. With this, I entered yet another world I had never experienced.

Free to come and go, I found a job to help pay the rent and spent my nights getting high and experiencing whatever adventure the night would bring. Having lived within a world of criticism and control, I felt finally free to make decisions of my own. This would lead to a dark world—a world of watching and experiencing the pain of others, others like me who were lost inside the dark thoughts of their minds, clueless as to who they were and seeking for something, anything to cling to. Though I didn't know it then, this experience would later build within me a compassion and understanding of the lost. At the time, though, I was one with them, lost inside my own dark thoughts.

During this time, I was introduced to heroin. I found it to be a lovely drug, as, once high, all the cares of my world left my mind, allowing me to rest in peace, a peace I had not had since I was a little child. The girl who had introduced me to this drug took me to a local "shooting gallery" to "score" our daily high, where I was led deeper into this very different world. On the steps leading up to the room where we were to meet the dealer were many people, either already stoned or shooting up right there on the steps, eager to escape their pain.

In the dealer's room, I discovered a heavy darkness unlike anything I had ever experienced, as his "girls" would enter after their night on the street to give him their earnings. Stoned myself, I watched as one young, extremely beautiful girl was beaten and dragged across the room by her hair, as she had not "earned your keep." Crying and screaming, she promised to do better, wanting only her fix to escape her pain.

This was a turning point in my use of heroin. Already on the road to dependence myself, I made the decision right then to go the other way, as I did not want to end up like the poor girl I had just seen beaten and abused. As I walked out of that room, I was free from the use of this mind-numbing drug that held so many captive.

This did not end a period of being introduced to other drugs, sexual exploits, new faces, and travel. Moving from place to place, traveling to the West Coast and back home again, I soon became exhausted. Tired, always hungry, and seeing no end in sight, I made the decision that I was done with this new life and called home, ready to return.

Like the prodigal child, I was welcomed with open arms. But behind my mother's back a whip was hidden, ready to strike. That would come out later. Once home, I ate ravenously; slept for hours on a comfortable bed, instead of a sleeping bag on the floor; and made every attempt to keep my experiences to myself. Not that anyone ever asked or seemed to care, as they didn't want to hear.

Beginning to physically heal, I was daily reminded that I was still the rebel, the black sheep. The reminders were there every day of what a disappointment I had become. Here, the whip came out, and the barbs at the end were razor-sharp points of criticism, judgment, and condemnation for who I was and what I had done. Each strike embedded the poison of guilt deeply into the wounds, guilt that would fester and infect, leaving me limp and in pain. I made no effort to stop the beating, as, by then, I felt I deserved every strike of the whip; the fight left me, and I would succumb to the life she desired of me.

It was here that I fell into the very box I had been running from so long. My only thought, at the time, was to redeem myself from this image she held of a very unlikeable, unacceptable, and most unworthy girl.

It was here that I made the decision to make no decisions for myself ever again. I was told that my decisions were failures, and I had begun to feel like a failure myself. At that time, I believed I was incapable of making decisions that would benefit me or bring to me the freedom I desired, and I was tired and weary. So I made one last decision of my own and placed my life in my mother's hands to lead. Maybe this time, with someone other than myself to lead the way, my life would be different, and I would be accepted. Perhaps, if I only became what she expected, I would be pleasing enough and good enough to be valued and liked enough to belong. Although I would like to say this left me in peace, this decision to make no decision—a decision I would hold tightly to for most of my life—only left me feeling defeated, apathetic and without hope.

Remembering and seeing my seemingly fruitless search for freedom left me with an empty feeling of sadness. Thoughts of *if only things had been different, if only I had been accepted for who I was, if only someone had bothered to get to know me* kept running through my mind. Yet here, as always, I was told to look again—this time free from the ideas, the beliefs, the judgments, and the labels held against me. Hearing these words, what I had been looking at began to shift and change. And when I looked again, it was like watching someone else. I could look at this young teenage girl with new eyes. As I watched, I saw a young girl seeking to find her true self boldly and bravely, giving no thought to fear or harm, only embracing a sense of adventure and excitement in the experience of being free to finally be.

Suddenly, there was no question in my mind as to why I'd done the things that I'd done. This was why I am here—to be free and experience this freedom in all that came my way. Whatever came up, I was game to try, liking some, choosing not to try others ever again, but no fear in the trying. The only times I remember feeling fear was when others tried to put me in a box of their making, and I felt I had to fight for my life, or lose it forever, as those within this box appeared to be smothered, lifeless, and without hope. This was no place I wanted to live and what I would continue to run from. What a new revelation, helping me to be aware of how brave and courageous I am, ready to experience each new adventure with excitement. And I wanted her back!

It was here that I saw that the only mistake I made was allowing fear to enter in when I returned. It was not the fear of the adventures but fear of being an outcast, of not belonging, and of losing the acceptance of others. Accepting this fear, I was entering a realm where I buried my true self and began to resist the brave essence of who I am in my attempt to fit it and be "like them." The true me was not, and I am not, "like them," but I hid myself to become like them and lost myself. As an imposter, I was about to live a miserable existence denying the truth of who I am.

Looking back from this new perspective, I saw my past experiences were mine to shape and mold me; to make me strong and resilient, knowledgeable and wise, understanding and compassionate; and to prepare me for the life I was to live ahead in serving others. For now I understood and could not condemn, having been there and done that. While this was a world frowned upon, judged by others, now I knew that, damn, I've lived, while others have merely followed in the footsteps of others, wondering if this was what life is all about. Beginning to sense a new high, an inner high more beautiful than words can describe, it was here in this chapter of my life review that a new beginning of total and complete acceptance for who I am began.

Feeling free in this moment, it was time to move on, knowing there was so much more truth to find. By now, I was curious as to who I would find, as my thoughts about myself were rapidly changing. I was beginning to see who I truly am and what had really happened, and my life was being transformed by this new sight.

Chapter 6

LOOKING FOR LOVE IN ALL THE WRONG PLACES ... UNDER EVERY ROCK!

The farther backward you can look,
the farther ahead you can see.

—Winston Churchill

*O*nce returning home and after a slow recovery, it was time to move on, but where? While my mother had backed off from her continual tirade of what I was doing wrong, the pressure continued to follow the path she had in mind for me. In an effort to get her off my emotional back, I reenrolled in high school with enough credits to start my final year of school in the fall, so the pressure was temporarily off. It felt good to be back in a routine, and I slipped easily back into the straight A average I'd always held and would soon graduate. Slipping back into the neighborhood gang came easily as well.

While I had been gone, a guy I knew from the neighborhood had moved back in with his mother just down the road. He was known as "the Hunk," as he was tall, well-muscled, very handsome, and a charmer. We began to hang out, and it soon became a full-blown sex fest. It wasn't long before he became jealous and possessive, insisting on driving me to school and back home to make sure I was not talking with anyone else while I was away. We were together always when I was not in school, and my family loved him. Not only was he from the old neighborhood, but my sister and brother had gone to school with his father and uncles, and he hunted, fished, played cards, and fit right into the family traditions.

While he was charming in the beginning, it wasn't long before the verbal abuse began. Loving and attentive in front of my family, he changed when we were alone, making sure I knew he was in control. He battered my self-esteem with labels of *slut* and *whore*, telling me the only reason he was with me was because he felt sorry for me and that no one else would touch a slut like me. The words hurt. But to me, they rang true, reinforcing my thoughts of myself at the time of being worthless and of no value.

I endured the abuse, partly because, after all, he was the hunk that all the other girls wanted and I now had, but mainly because my family loved him, earning me their approval at long last. This went on for almost two years, as he integrated into the family and appeared to all as the loving boyfriend. Plans for marriage were in my family's mind. They hoped to finally get me settled and "normal" with this "nice" boy. Yet, this was not my plan, as it came with intense fear.

Having just enough self-esteem left, I knew that I could not, would not live with this abuse for the rest of my life. So I slowly and cautiously began to withdraw. When I finally broke free, all hell broke loose, both from him and my family. He began to threaten me with physical violence if I did not return, and my family had turned their backs, once again, on this rebel who never fit in. When he saw that his threats were not winning me back, he chose another tactic. Gentle, persuasive, and kind, he asked me to go out with him one last time, so that he could show me a good time and prove that he could change. Reluctantly and unwisely, I finally agreed.

By ignoring my instincts, I was to learn that I had made a huge mistake. We went out, hung out with friends, and then I was ready to go home. On the way back, he again began his verbal abuse, only it was more heated and uglier than ever before. Passing a diner, I asked to stop, with the excuse that I needed to use the bathroom. Once inside, I called and asked my mother to come and pick me up. But halfway through the call, he came in yelling, grabbed me by the hair, and dragged me back into his car.

We didn't go home. Instead, he drove to an isolated location in the country, and under threat of torture and lighting me on fire to burn, I endured hours of rape. When he finally took me home, literally shoving me out of the car, I ran in the house sobbing and shaking and told my mother what had happened. Knowing we had been having sex throughout our relationship, she sneered and, laughing, walked away, leaving me crying. It was never mentioned again, as no one wanted to hear.

Because I was now out of school and home, with him still living down the road, I slept with a loaded shotgun next to the door when my mother went to work. If he had dared come to the door and try to force his way in, I would have shot him with no regrets. Thankfully, he did not.

Beginning to emotionally heal once again, I found a good job and my own place and began to go out with friends on the weekends. One night, I met a quiet guy who was soft-spoken with a great smile and we began to go out. While nothing like the abuser from before, he was as dysfunctional as the rest. But of course, so was I, and like attracts like. We moved in together.

Already a heavy drinker, he began to lose himself in the booze and drugs. One night, sitting around with a bunch of friends, someone brought over some cocaine, and it was shared by all. Unknown by anyone, this cocaine was cut with a tranquilizer, and I got a full dose. As I sat next to my boyfriend, I realized I couldn't move, and with lips that would barely open, I told him that I needed help. As he tried to help me stand, I collapsed in a heap. Thankfully, someone there saw what was happening and was familiar with drug overdoses, so he and my boyfriend carried me outside and walked me up and down the driveway in the winter cold until I began to come around. This was my second near drug overdose, having experienced a similar episode out West a few years before. This was a wake-up call for me. It was time to walk away from the relationship and back to my own place to try and start again.

Finally fed up with losers, and knowing this rat race had to end, I dated no one for a long time. One night, at an elegant company party, the CEO of the company approached me to dance, and I was flattered. We later left together and had wild, crazy sex in a rented room. He was hooked, but I was not, as he was married. So I began to avoid him at work. This did not deter him, and the pursuit began in earnest. Slowly, persistently, he persuaded me to go out for dinner or drinks. It was casual conversation that drew me in, as I found him enjoyable and comfortable to talk with. He had come from a similar background as mine, with many of the same values I had been brought up with.

After four or five months, we were together every time he could get away, often traveling out of town. This led to four years of new experiences and places I had never seen or been to before throughout the country, years filled with elegant dinners, attending plays, and visiting another new and unknown world. This new life also came with a lot of alone time. I filled the gaps with trips with new friends I met along the way, women in the same situation as I was in, waiting around for a married man to find time for us.

Then, one day he showed up to tell me he'd left his wife the night before. Now he and I could forever be together. My mind swirled, my breath was knocked out of me, and I realized suddenly that, for me, this had been a safe relationship, one in which I did not have to worry about a commitment to anyone. And I ran, not asking myself where I was running to and not looking back.

It would be back to the familiar. By then, I had a new job, earning great pay, and could well afford to travel with friends on the weekends and just simply be free. Within this new job, I worked for a beautiful, rich, and educated woman, who took me under her wing and taught me how to dress in style; to act like a sophisticated, elegant lady; and to wear makeup, which she bought for me from New York and Paris. We enjoyed each other's company and began going out after work often. The friendship began to come to an end when, one night, she shared with me that she had fallen in love with me and that her husband would turn her on during sex by talking about what I was doing to her instead of him. Asking me to travel with her and her husband to other states and countries, she promised to show me the world. Again, I ran. And, again, as always, I didn't ask myself where I was running to, just away.

Tiring of living alone, I began sharing an apartment with an old neighborhood friend and was back to the bar scene. One morning, I woke up to my roommate in tears, telling me how she had come home from work the night before to find me lying naked on my bed, comatose, and barely breathing, and she could not wake me. She shared how she could tell that others had been in the apartment, as the place appeared ransacked, with everything out of place, but I remembered nothing. As I left for work, I couldn't even find my car, finally finding it parked in an unfamiliar place where I would never have parked it. Obviously, someone had driven me home, but I had no idea who. Later, I would find out that I had been slipped a date rape drug at the bar, leaving me with no memory of what had happened. Fear overwhelmed me and I hit an all-time low. Tired of running, tired of getting drunk and high every night and tired of being afraid of what was coming next, I knew I needed help, but I was clueless where to turn or where to go to find it.

As my divine intervention would have it, a relative was in town visiting her mother, and I went to visit them. It would be through this chance occurrence that I was to find the help I was looking for and from a very unexpected place.

It was here, in this chapter, that I could see that I was never alone. With all the bizarre situations that I have gotten myself into, I was always led out safely. Perhaps a bit bruised and banged up, I always had a chance to heal before again jumping into another unknown situation that my passion for discovery and freedom was leading me to. Curious about life all my life, I could now see I wanted to know and experience it all. The one truth I had to learn, that I did not learn until I looked back, was that I had always been protected and only experienced what I would later use to help others who had taken a similar blind path based on false thoughts about their true selves.

Never again would I doubt that things happened for a reason, reasons we do not see until we look back. There was a plan for me, a purpose unknown to me at the time. And I had always been where I was meant to be to become fully who I am—learning what I want; what I don't want; and, best of all, to do what I am here to do, and that is to share the hidden truth within every experience. Now I knew that my heart had always heard the inner guidance, even though my lost mind had not, for I had survived and would thrive.

With this life review far from over, for there is so much more to see, I found that I now had a newfound confidence, a confidence that came from knowing I'd never been alone, never forsaken and always loved for who I am, safe within an unseen, unknown embrace. Within this confidence, I could now walk forward with a greater peace to find more treasures of truth that lay ahead to be found in looking back.

Chapter 7

NEW BEGINNINGS:
LOST OR FOUND?

*We often avoid our destiny out of a sense of
obligation we've been taught to follow.*

—self-reflection

When I was visiting with my relatives, they shared about a co-pastor team of husband and wife who taught weekly Bible studies at a nearby location. Having checked it out, they found the teaching charismatic and powerful and invited me to go with them to their church the following Sunday and listen for myself. When I heard the word "church," my first thought was, *You have to be shitting me*, and I declined their invitation.

The following week, they invited me again. Hoping to get them off my back, I agreed to go. In total rebel style, I wore tattered jeans; boots; and a tight, revealing top with no bra. Following them in through the door, I saw there were greeters on each side. One greeter gave me a beaming smile and big hug and, looking me in the eye, didn't even seem to see what I wore. Not a hugger myself,

I expected repulsion, but all I felt was warmth. Sitting through the morning meeting, I was barely listening but observing everything and everyone around me. There were no looks of rejection or criticism sent my way, no stares, and no reproach for how I had chosen to appear. So I relaxed and soaked in warm acceptance.

The following Sunday I joined my aunt and cousin again and, like the week before, experienced nothing but a warm, genuine welcome and acceptance from those around me. The third Sunday, my aunt and cousin decided not to attend, and I was devastated! Reaching deep within me for strength and courage, I made the decision to go alone. This time, I dressed a bit more respectfully, as I was entering the lion's den alone and needed all the reassurance I could muster. Those in attendance saw me enter by myself and made every effort to make me feel welcome and at home among them. And by the time I left, I was hooked.

Soon attending every Sunday, I eventually began to attend their midweek teachings as well. The wife was vibrant, exciting, and powerful, and I was drawn to her. Eventually, she took me under her wing for one-on-one conversations. One Sunday, I responded to the call to come forward and "be saved and filled with the Holy Spirit." Having no idea what this entailed, never having heard this invitation before, I decided, if this was what they were offering, I wanted whatever they had. Afterward, everyone in attendance gave me hugs and words of welcome, and a new life began.

As time went on, the wife asked me to help with weekly duties, and I felt very grateful and happy to have been singled out and asked to assist. Afterward, we would talk, and she shared that she would like to use me to help in other ways. But to do so, they had requirements. The helpers could not smoke or drink. At the time, I was still doing both, and this presented a serious decision on my part. Could I, would I give up my previous lifestyle completely? But, seriously, what did I have to lose? The old way, or the new way, the old fear and trouble I had lived in, or the love and acceptance I had found here? The decision came easily. Within a week, the cigarettes and booze were out of my life, and a new experience had truly begun.

Around this same time, I ran into my old boyfriend, who I had lived with for a short while. I was taking a walk on my lunch break from work when we passed on the street, and he paused when he saw me. I didn't recognize him, as he had lost a lot of weight; he told me who he was and shared that he was now doing well and had left the past behind. He asked me to join him for lunch the following day, and he shared his story of what had occurred after I'd left.

In a drunken rage, he'd confronted one of the men we had hung out with, accusing him of breaking the two of us up. He had a gun with him, but when he pulled the trigger, it had jammed and did not fire. When he sobered up, he was full of fear at what he had almost done and drove himself to the closest AA meeting hall he could find. There he sobered up; learned the twelve steps; and met new, sober friends. His life was totally changed.

Impressed, I shared with him my own lifestyle change, and it seemed to both of us that we were meant to be together again. Eventually, I began attending his AA meetings with him. There he would give his "testimony" of losing me and finding sobriety, which had led him back to me; he now knew that it was with me that he was meant to stay. His testimony was warming and inspiring to all in attendance, including me.

Meeting his new friends, I saw how supportive and encouraging they were to one another, and I met his sponsor as well. The sponsor was homosexual, with partners coming and going, but this did not faze me in the least. By now, I'd been around every type of person one could imagine and was accepting of one and all.

My friend and I were together for five or six months before I shared this new relationship with my pastor. As I confided in her about my relationship and the people I was meeting, she was silent before telling me there was only one true way to God; AA was the devil's detour away from true salvation; and that homosexuality was an abomination to God, and all who participated in such devilish acts must be avoided at all costs for fear of eternal hell. Although none of this felt right, I adored her and, in my adoration, chose to believe her.

That night, I went to my friend, explaining what I had learned and asked him to attend my church with me, hoping to draw him away from the danger he was in. He adamantly refused, telling me had found his way; it was working for him successfully, and he needed no other way. After that, we began to disagree and argue, with me judging how he was living and him fighting against my judgment. It wasn't long before we went our separate ways, with hard feelings between the two of us caused by the judgment I was being taught and was now living by.

Settling deeper into this new life, I was now actively involved in helping out at church and meeting new friends who had joined, with similar backgrounds as mine, and we were traveling around the state to listen to various speakers and meeting at each other's houses. It was like one big happy family, and I felt I finally belonged and had found my true home.

As my church involvement grew, so did my desire for the Bible. For hours at a time, I devoured it, reading it through more times than I can recall. It wasn't long before I could quote scripture by heart with chapter and verse. Hungry for truth, I could not get enough of this new food to my heart and mind. As I sat reading the Bible alone at home one night, I heard what sounded like a voice in my head say, *God is Love. If it isn't Love, it isn't God.* It was so clear that it startled me, and I sat and thought about what I had heard for a long time.

When I went back to reading, the words had taken on a whole new meaning, and all I saw was love. Before, I had been reading the Bible based on the teachings I was receiving at church, and I had believed all I heard. Interwoven throughout these teachings was a lot of judgment against other religions, faiths, cultures, sexual preferences, and people who did not walk as we walked—in the "true way," as it was called. After hearing these words about love, I began to question these teachings, as judgment did not sound like love to me at all, and I took my questions to my pastor.

She was not pleased with my questioning, informing me that I was not to question, as she was ordained by God to speak the truth, and I was simply to listen and believe. She believed in a God of righteous judgment, who condemned the sinner until the sinner spoke a few magic words to Jesus, and that was the only way to "be saved" from God's wrath.

But I did question, as I did not want to judge, and her answer did not satisfy or align with what I now knew I had heard directly from this Source of love. This created a silent distrust between us, unspoken but both of us knowing it was there. Although I was unaware, she began to devise a plan to keep me where she was sure I belonged, which was safe with her. She became determined to find someone within our church for me to marry, thereby keeping me from wandering too far.

At age twenty-nine, I had no thought of marriage, as I believed that I had found my home, had very close friends within the church that I enjoyed, and desired no man to fulfill me. There were few single men in my church and no one that interested me, as I was not looking. One night after the midweek teaching, my pastor led me over to a new group of young men who had been attending. Saying to them, "There is someone I want you to meet," she literally shoved me into their group.

Confused and embarrassed, I introduced myself. They introduced themselves to me, and one young man in particular was especially friendly, making me later wonder if he had been talked to before this meeting had occurred. It wasn't long before I knew he had, as he began to pursue a relationship. My pastor did her part, encouraging me to get to know this young man better, explaining that he had a pastor's heart, and perhaps we were meant to be together to build a ministry. Planting her seeds in my mind, praying they would take root, and knowing that I was all for God with a natural ability to teach, she hoped that I would begin to consider the possibility.

Yet, I was torn and unsure. While I could see the possibility, he was younger than me, and I did not love him or feel attracted to him. Still, as time went on, and we began to get to know each other, I could see his calling, his strength, and his love of God. We began to draw closer. Mistaking this as love for him, not realizing that I was attracted to the love within him, the same love that was in me, I ignored the voice of caution speaking within me and began following my pastor's plan.

Within a few months, we were engaged to be married. My family, although questioning, accepted my decision, hoping that, at long last, I was to settle down and be normal. After all, I was twenty-nine years old, never married, and had caused them many years of discomfort and fear for my well-being. Plans began and it wasn't long before the wedding was to be a reality. Still unsettled and feeling no attraction for this man, it was only the thought of a ministry and my growing friendship with him that gave me any peace. After all, a woman that I admired and trusted was encouraging this decision and was telling me it was the will of God. So, we married.

After the wedding, he moved in with me, as I had my own home by then, and we were left to adjust to our new life together. Of course, sex came into play, and I found myself unsatisfied and unfilled in this aspect of our life. My sexual experiences in the past had been based primarily on the chase, the thrill of conquest, and the freedom to leave at will. Here, in marriage, I experienced no thrill and no sense of excitement, and routine lovemaking held no pleasure for me, only a sense of duty and obligation. He sensed my disappointment but was a man who longed to please and tried in every way he could conceive of, while I simply tolerated. Too late, I would recognize that, with no love, there was no attraction, and with no attraction, there could be no fulfillment. It was too late, as I was married, fulfilling the will of another but not my own.

Leaving this aspect of our life at home, we both totally submerged ourselves in the church. My pastor was overjoyed to have gotten her way and made every attempt to offer us opportunities to become an established fixture within her church. Yet, I still had this gnawing discomfort at the teaching I was hearing, and I had a deep longing to find this God of love I had met the year before. As my longing grew, so did my search for a way out—a way that would be pleasing and acceptable to both my pastor and my new husband.

And a then a plan came to mind. We would leave this church and attend the training center where my pastors had graduated from, which was miles away. I presented this to my husband, and he agreed and began to get excited. Together, we went to our pastors and shared with them our desire to leave and go to school and get our certification, promising to return and enrich our church. This was met with disappointment at our leaving. But with their blessing, we enrolled and would be expected the coming fall.

The evening of the final service at our church, I sat and sobbed alone in our car in the parking lot, as I knew I didn't really want to go so far away to school and that it had been a desperate plan devised to escape the snare I felt wrapped around me. But I had now ensnared myself, and I saw no way out, other than to proceed forward on the plan that was mine in the first place. As in the past, I was running again.

Quite a bit was revealed to me here. The first was that I'd find what I was expecting to find. Having long expected judgment, I was always trying to avoid it by following another's will for my life instead of my own. This only resulted in receiving my own self-judgment for my own choice. Had this worked? Obviously not, for I could see that, in trying to avoid judgment, I was always denying myself and living a miserable existence. It was past time to ask myself the only question that matters: What is it that *I* want? What am *I* searching for? If I wasn't conscious in my search of what I wanted, then I'd continue running from what I didn't want. Asking myself what it was that I truly wanted and was searching for, the answer was clear. What I wanted above all else was to find my true self and stop following what others want of me.

With this question answered, I was prompted to look at this time period again. As I did, I saw another picture. This picture was totally different than the one I had long been focused on. Sitting and really looking at this new picture, I started to smile. Before me, I again saw an adventurer, fully aware and simply bored with the adventure I had been on. Ready for something new, having already found the treasure of truth that I had been searching for, it was time to move on to the next. Literally laughing out loud, I could see that I had not been running from anything but, rather, running toward the next new adventure into truth!

With a very different and more liberated view of myself, I felt lighter and freer, ready to move on to see what other surprises lay ahead, buried far too long from my sight.

Chapter 8

ANOTHER JOURNEY: NOT SURE WHERE, BUT WHAT THE HELL?!

*When an inner situation is not made
conscious, it appears outside as fate.*

—Carl Jung

There was much to do before the move was made, with jobs to turn into the hands of another, belongings to pack, and goodbyes to be made. The day of the move, I was feeling a bit lighter and looking forward to a new adventure. With everything packed, my mother arrived, not to say goodbye but to send me off in her usual style. She stood in the driveway, arms crossed, lips pinched, and eyes narrowed. The hug and kiss I offered were met with stone-faced refusal to acknowledge my presence. This image would follow me to my new destination.

We finally arrived, settled into our apartment, looked for jobs, and then it was time to enroll in school. This was actually a magical place for both of us, as we had read all the founder's books. And here we were smack-dab in the middle of it all. Between work and school, our lives were busy. We made few friends there, depending on each other for company in the small amount of downtime we found. In most cases, this experience would draw two people closer together, but it did not and through no fault of my new husband, as it was all me. Now knowing that I made the mistake of marrying him to please another and having no romantic love for him, I kept him at a distance and buried myself in keeping busy. Along with this resistance was the image scorched in my thoughts of my mother, always scowling, always disapproving and judging. The time away would not erase it. My calls home that year were met with either silence or an abrupt yes or no to always end short. She never called me.

Despite both of us doing well in school and at our jobs, if not in our relationship, it was not enough to keep me there. At the end of our first year, I told my husband that I could not stay another year to graduate, as I was ready to return home. As always, he didn't question and was very understanding, so we sold our belongings to obtain the money needed for the drive home, loaded up, and headed for home to live with my parents until we could find jobs and a place of our own.

The homecoming was not joyful, as my mother greeted us at the door with a smirk and an "I told you so" look in her eyes. Neither was it easy living with her, as she still had her routine, and our being there was not part of it. Any attempt on my part to help clean or cook was met with angry resentment, resulting in the slinging of unkind words that would leave me in tears. I spent a lot of time alone in my room crying.

My husband had found a job, while I helped my niece by caring for her children while she worked, and I was left at home with my mother. After a very short time, my mother had had enough of us being there and had found, and purchased, a small trailer for us in a nearby trailer park. Informing us of what she had done, she made it clear it was time to move, and I cannot say I was disappointed to leave.

When we returned home, we had settled back in at the church we had left and were joyfully welcomed back. Still feeling reservations toward my pastor, I settled in with little enthusiasm. Big plans were made for my husband, and he was soon being groomed to teach and was excited to begin. His first night going solo, we were both looking forward to it. I made plans to join him, sitting in the back to encourage and enjoy his first teaching gig. My pastor had other plans.

As I began to follow him into the room, I was told no, that I was not to be allowed to sit in, as I would be a distraction; this was something he must do on his own. Hearing this, I was furious, beyond furious, and I was filled with resentment and anger at her decision, although I didn't say a word. It was at that point that I knew it was time to leave for good. Now I just had to figure out how to unwrap the tentacles again forming around us to make the escape.

By now, my husband and I were working and making the best of things. Well, he was. Always easygoing and fun loving, he could be at home and comfortable anywhere he happened to be. But I was still struggling with my thoughts of resistance; my mother's judgment; and our pastor's firm, controlling hand. Thankfully, there were light times as well, helping to balance my thoughts, as I had many friends, old and new. We had company over often, and life was again pretty full.

One evening, we had my parents over for dinner and, after dinner, my mother said that she and my father had something to talk with us about. What came next was a total shock. She had decided it was time for the two of them to downsize and move to a smaller house in preparation for my father's upcoming retirement. Her plan was for the two of us to move into their old house when they moved, and she offered us minimal payments. There was an immediate no on my lips. But before I could speak, my husband, excited at this unexpected gift, said yes. My gut wrenched. Inwardly, I continued saying, *No, no, no.* I did not want to return to the house where I had grown up, filled with unhappy memories and years of judgment and pain. Too late, as I had not said a word and would, once again, follow the decisions of others for my life. There was a foreboding of what was to come, and none of it was good. My thoughts were too full of resentment, dwelling on the past. For me, life was not moving in a positive direction, yet I was not strong or courageous enough to stand up and speak.

Now feeling trapped in a house where I did not want to be, I turned my focus on finding a way out of our current church. Having heard about another local church, I asked my husband to go to a midweek service, as we had to be discreet. We went, and both of us felt comfortable and enjoyed both the teaching and meeting the pastor and his associates. It wasn't long before we agreed to switch to this new church. Our leaving the old was not pleasant, but I no longer cared. In the new church, my husband was soon pulled into the teaching ministry, while I was offered a secretarial position working within the church office. Soon, I was working in the office, interacting daily with the pastor. While the position appeared ideal, I soon found that it had its downside, as I heard too much. The man I heard teaching from the stage was not the same man behind closed doors, and my judgment began to bloom. Once again, I began to make plans to escape, as this was not what I had been searching for, being unable to see around the judgment I had planted in my mind and had allowed to grow.

As I had never being good at hiding my feelings, my judgmental thoughts were soon sensed, so my husband and I made the decision to meet with the pastor and discuss our future there. Our meeting was diplomatic and restrained, and the suggestion was made for the two of us to form our own church, which was a nice way of getting rid of us—or, should I say, me. Upon his suggestion, we mortgaged our home and proceeded to form our own church.

We selected a church name with the motto "where the truth is spoken in love." Having had enough of the judgment and condemnation I had heard in the other churches, I was ready to share the God that I had found and fallen in love with, the God of Love. Our little congregation began to grow, and we were excited and again very busy.

Meanwhile at home, I was watching my father die within. He had not wanted to leave his home and move into this tiny house, a house where my mother had moved him into his own room, no longer wanting to be in the same room with him at night. Now that he was retired, he was spending every day with my mother, in her way and hearing about it daily. Watching, I understood that he could barely breathe for fear of criticism. He was living in a toxic environment, inhaling it every day. He had never been one to speak up for himself, and there was nothing I could do as I watched him lose the will to live. A few months later, he died of a massive heart attack. Dad had finally made his escape.

After this occurred, my sister's bitterness and resentment flamed toward our mother, as she blamed our father's death on her. Her words and actions were increasingly sharp and critical, and she withdrew any emotional support, leaving our mother increasingly emotionally dependent on me. Between this new burden, my continued resistance to my marriage, and dealing with my own inner bitterness and resentment, a toll was being taken on our church. The numbers slowly dwindled, debt was rising, and we soon made the decision to close the doors.

Back to finding jobs, for me life went on, and I was unaware of the damage that closing our church had had on my husband. Never once in our marriage had we ever talked about our relationship, our dreams, our desires, and where we were going. And we didn't now. Too late, I would see that his dreams had come crashing down around him. And finding no solace at home, he was seeking his own way out of what he was coming to find intolerable.

One day while I was at work, he called to tell me he had moved out of our home and was living elsewhere. Speechless, frozen, and dumbstruck at his words, I was screaming inside, *You can't leave me. I am your wife.*

But he had, and I went home to find the house empty of his belongings. The pain felt unbearable. I curled up on the couch unable to move as our past flashed through my mind, a past now filled with debilitating guilt. For weeks afterward, I withdrew, making an appearance at work and nothing more.

Refusing to believe he was gone forever, when the knock came on the door and a stranger handed me divorce papers to sign, I experienced a sense of rejection that was overwhelming. Guilt exploded in my mind, as I had had plenty of time alone to look back and see what I had been doing. This guilt began to consume and devour me; I had listened to another and had married him for all the wrong reasons and then put all the blame on him.

There was so much bitterness and resentment within me during this period of my life. Everywhere I turned, it seemed like someone was trying to control me or change me or refusing to listen to me, which only increased the blame I had boiling inside of me. It was with a jolt of recognition that I saw that both my sister and I had been walking in our mother's footsteps, thinking her thoughts of blame and judgment, unable to find our own true thoughts. All of this bitterness and resentment, a need for some kind of control, were all thoughts we had grown up with and learned. Focusing on this period of my life, I asked myself, Where were *my* own thoughts? It was now easy to see that they were buried under years of learned wrong thinking.

Wanting to know the truth of the many lessons found here, I looked closer and, once again, saw a whole different picture. This new view showed me that all those I had judged were just doing the best they knew how with the knowledge they had, sometimes making good decisions that benefitted themselves and others, sometimes not so good for either one. With past judgment slowly dissipating, I saw the pastors I had judged in a new and different way, recognizing their strengths; their weaknesses; and, most of all, their desire to truly serve the God they loved. They were no different than me, with pasts that had influenced their thoughts in ways that often brought out the best, and the worst, in all of us. Who was I to judge with all the mistakes I had made, mistakes I now knew had taught me so much of what to do and what not to do. Weren't they the same? Oh yes.

There was more to see here. They say that silence is golden, but in silencing my voice long ago, I had hurt not only myself, but also those around me. If I was ever to be free, I had to release myself of this fear to speak what was in my heart and learn how to be honest and straightforward in my relationships and, most importantly, with myself. Even as I saw this truth, it came with great fear. But there was also a knowing that I would be shown where this courage would come from to release me from such an ancient fear.

It would take me many months to assimilate and begin to apply all that I had seen here, and I was thankful for the inner help I received. Never alone, I would continue on, seeking the truth and, in being shown, allowing the truth to replace the lies that for too long had influenced my every thought.

While the truth can hurt, it is so liberating at the same time. And I now knew I no longer wanted to follow the path I had been on and was still following in this moment in my life. With my vision beginning to clear, another limiting belief from my past had disappeared, and peace and self-acceptance settled more deeply within me. I was ready to go on, to continuing clearing the way of all the mental barriers from the past that had been holding me back from living the life I was here to live. A new door was opening, and it was up to me to step into my future.

Chapter 9

CHOOSE WRONG?
CHOOSE AGAIN!

The road to hell is paved with good intentions.

—Henry G. Bohn / Proverbs

Full of pain, I settled into a new routine of work, tending to my home, yard, and many rescued cats. While I'd been married, stray cats had begun to appear around our home, always gaunt and starving, seeking shelter. Taking them in, getting them healthy and altered, and watching them thrive while finding good, loving homes was rich and rewarding. Their constant companionship and love were comforting to me during this time. Alone again, I began to write once more. Writing was a place to record my pain, my questions, and my search for answers and to try to gain a sense of understanding as I tried to figure out what the hell was going on with my life. I lost a lot of weight, and my stomach was always tied up in knots. A new body began to emerge, one that was attractive and appealing as I would later find out. With my mother living down the street, I spent more time with her to make sure she was faring well without my dad, and she was. Free from the burden of marriage, she had made a few new friends in her neighborhood.

Still working full time, I had several new friends and we began to go out for dinner occasionally. Life began to feel normal again, and I was beginning to heal. The company I worked with had a catastrophe unit that would fly staff out all over the states to handle insurance claims wherever any kind of natural disaster would occur. As I was now single, I was asked if I was interested in joining this unit and going out for a week or two to process claims onsite. Sure, why not? This was something new and different. My first assignment was hectic. The work was demanding and exhilarating, occupying my time and mind, and I met many new people from all over the United States.

As I handled the job well, I was asked to go more and more often and so, leaving my responsibilities at home to my mother and several willing friends, I was free to fly wherever the service was needed. These were fun and exciting times, visiting states I had never been to before, meeting people from many different walks of life, making friends, and partying at night when the work was done for the day. There was no time to think about the past and only the moment to enjoy, and I thrived in this environment for several years.

At home during downtime, I went back to my regular position at work, taking care of responsibilities at home, going out occasionally with friends, and writing. Life was beginning to feel rich and meaningful again. Out with a friend at a pub one night, I ran into a guy that I'd had a crush on in ninth grade, although we had never gotten together. Standing at the bar, he was alone, so I went up, said hi, caught up for a moment, and went back to my friends. One day, while I was outside working in my yard, he drove by and stopped. We chatted a moment, and he drove on. I didn't think much about it. That winter, I returned home from work and found a single rose in a vase with a simple note saying, "Just thinking about you." It was from my old classmate, and I found it sweet and thoughtful. A few months later, he called, and we talked for a short while, catching up again. We said goodbye, and that was it. He began pursuing in earnest that summer.

None of my friends were picking up good vibes from this new friend. He was a loner, had no friends, didn't mingle well with others, and would be short and abrupt with others' advances toward friendship, as his attention was solely focused on me. They began to warn me to be careful. Red flags were going up all around us—seen only by them. All I saw was a lonely man seeking companionship who had chosen me, just another stray seeking comfort and security with someone who cared. Soon, he began consuming my time, calling, coming over and inviting me away from my friends to go somewhere to be alone with him, and I went.

Before long, he became possessive, proclaiming his love and telling me how he had been searching for me, the girl he had known in school, after all these years. During this time, he shared much about his life, filled with trauma and many losses, and my heart went out to him. It wasn't long before I became determined to show him the love he had never experienced, love that I had to give.

By the end of summer, he began to demand we marry, as he feared losing me again. While my mother and friends found this unsettling due to his possessiveness, I knew my love would save him from his troubled past, and we married. My mother refused to attend our simple wedding, as she did not like or trust him and had also grown accustomed to having me to herself, something she did not want to lose. After we'd married, he moved in with me, and our life together began.

In the beginning, I continued meeting with close friends. He refused to go, choosing instead to sit alone at home. After a very short time, he began to demand that I cut off my friendships, as I now belonged to him. At first, I resisted, as I loved and enjoyed my friends. But one night after I returned home, a huge fight ensued. He began to cry hysterically, saying he wanted his sweet, innocent girl back, the one he knew in school, wailing that he had lost her. In disgust, I went to bed. Angry, he came in and tipped the bed over with me in it. Choosing to ignore him, I went to the spare room and spread my blanket out on the floor, prepared to go to sleep and escape this crazy person. But he followed me, still crying hysterically and, kneeling beside me, began to choke me. When I was almost to the point of blacking out, he released his hands and, still sobbing, began to tell me how sorry he was, professing his undying love and begging for my forgiveness. When I could get up, I went into the living room and sat in a chair, my mind swirling with thoughts about what to do. The whole time he was kneeling beside me, overcome with fear and continuing his sobbing declarations of love.

Like a fool, I stayed. There was a voice in my thoughts telling me I could overcome this and still prove to this pitiful man he was worthy of love and that I could and would do this! It was the wrong voice.

Shortly afterward, I was called out by my unit to fly out west to work earthquake claims, and I went, glad to get away. We were busy, working twelve to fourteen hours a day, with claims piling up, phones ringing continuously, and my husband calling every hour. At first, he made the pretense of telling me he was calling to make sure that I was all right in this dangerous element I was in. Time and again, I would patiently explain that I was safe and very, very busy, ending with the promise that I would call him when I was able to get away in the evening.

This did not stop his calls, so I began hanging up on him. But once I was back in my hotel room, the phone would begin ringing again. At first, I took the calls, attempting to reassure him and let him know I would be home as soon as the job was done. We would hang up, and fifteen minutes later, he would call again. Finally, in desperation to sleep before another busy day began, I took the phone off the hook. The hotel office called me the next day to let me know that the calls continued to pour in throughout the night and asked what would I like them to do. Embarrassed, both in front of them and with my coworkers during the day, I explained that my husband was troubled for my safety, and I would take care of the problem.

After two weeks, the calls subsided, and I found out that he had decided to redo our bathroom at home to surprise me when I returned. Thankfully, he had found an outlet for his obsessive jealousy by tearing out walls, most likely envisioning me instead of walls.

When I returned home, my husband acted like nothing had happened. He was excited to show me the new bathroom he had completed in my absence, seeking my praise. And like with a little child, I gave it. At work, I put in my notice to the unit director, telling him that I could no longer travel as I had. He was devastated, as my work had excelled, and many words of thanks and written accolades had come pouring in for the excellent work we had done for all the companies we'd served. Needless to say, my boss didn't like my husband either. In truth, I knew no one who did, but I remained determined.

For another year, life went on with periods of calm, broken by extreme outbursts of rage and anger, and I learned to remain calm, as his outbursts never again resulted in physical violence. He would eventually regain his senses and always acted like the episode had never occurred. At work, I began staying late, not even wanting to return home, and the phone would ring over and over again. My body was experiencing great stress from the chaos at home, and I turned to a chiropractor in an attempt to ease the reoccurring headaches I was beginning to experience. While in her waiting room, I picked up a little blue book called *Heal Your Body* by Louise Hay and began to devour it. Later, I would be thankful for this brief encounter with the metaphysical, as it would begin to change my thoughts about life.

After a year and a half of marriage, I return home from work one day and found that my husband had moved all of his belongings out of the house, but he had waited to tell me that he was leaving and would not be returning. Even though our short life together had been hell, I was devastated, as another man was rejecting me, causing my thoughts to shout that I was worthless and a failure.

After he walked out the door for the final time, I crawled into a corner, curled up, and cried for hours—alone with only my own self-defeating thoughts.

Once again, I found this time painful to review, as I could see that my intentions had been good but convoluted and an attempt to redeem myself from the past. In treating my first husband so badly, I subconsciously felt that I had a debt to pay and must feel the same pain that I had inflicted on him. It had been guilt that had driven me into this second marriage, not the love I professed. This was a truth I needed to see, and I was seeing it now.

Also to be seen was the truth that I cannot save another who does not want to be saved. The desire to create a new way of living must come from within, as it is only then that one from without can help. And I saw myself again. No one and nothing could pull, push, or save me from myself, as it had to be my choice—my recognition that life could be different, better, richer, and fuller. That day was now at hand, as I was beginning to understand that only I could save me from my own imagined self.

Continuing to look at this picture painted before me, I also recognized an empath, one who takes on the pain of others, real or imagined, in whatever form it comes, be it a person, an animal, or worms on the playground. There was this need to save, to comfort, to help change the life of another living being, even at the sacrifice of my own. To be an empath is a gift but one to be used wisely. And I, as yet, did not have the wisdom to balance it with a sure foundation of who I am and what to do with the gift I had been given.

Further reflection here left me shaking my head, as I began to see that the combination of an empath and guilt was a sure road to disaster, and this was the road I had been traveling and would continue to travel until I could find my true self. Understanding that there were more pain-filled adventures ahead, I was beginning to see that this pain would one day lead me to the truth, as all pain can, once we have had enough of trying to blindly find the way ourselves. Willing to receive the truth I now knew I needed, I went on.

Chapter 10

HUNG A LEFT AND SHOULDA HUNG A RIGHT!

Almost all of our relationships begin, and most of
them continue, as forms of mutual exploitation,
a mental or physical barter, to be terminated
when one, or both parties, run out of goods.

—W. H. Auden

Left alone again, I found myself still sitting in a house where I did not want to live—a house filled with turmoil and strife; memories of an emotionally turbulent childhood containing rejection and blame; and, now, two failed marriages. Unable to see a way out of the web spun around me and unwilling to look too deeply into pain that was calling my name, I once again began to write. The truth wanted to be seen, and I was to be shown much through my writing in the days to come.

Blaming myself for the failure of my first marriage, I had entered the second to punish myself and atone for the pain I had caused in the first. But that was as far as I'd allowed pain to lead me. When the second divorce was final, I slowly accepted the fact that I had paid my debt and I hadn't lost much, except turmoil, drama, and walking on eggshells. The numbness and despair began to ease, and a lesson had been learned—that we can heal no one who does not want to be healed, especially when we are broken and bruised ourselves. Asking myself where to start this healing process, I had yet to see that the past had to be released and forgiven so I could be free now.

The more I wrote, the more I knew I just wanted to be free—free of relationships, of being who someone else wanted or needed me to be, of ongoing confusion about who or what I was and what I should be doing—and find some peace.

In my search for answers, I found myself led to a metaphysical bookstore in the area, and a whole new world opened. Here, I bought books, began attending classes, and found mentally exotic and stimulating experiences. The healing found in animal medicine was introduced to me. And in learning meditation, I went on delightful and revealing adventures with animal guides, which I would later discover were revealing my present and future to me.

One in particular still stands out. I saw myself as a young deer running through a raging forest fire, in which I had lost all that was near and dear to me, to emerge on the other side where I was safe, and although singed and burned, I was alive and free to begin again. Although I didn't realize it at the time, deer's message is the healing power of gentleness, and I was being told that I was coming to the edge of the forest and running from fear, death, and destruction of my very self and to be gentle with myself. Remembering this later— as, at that time, I was not out of the fire yet—I would see the truth in the message I had been given then. Yet even then, I felt a great sense of peace, and I sought more of what this new life had to offer.

With a new outlook on life, I was beginning to feel free to enjoy myself and my freedom again. Visiting relatives and friends; taking trips; and keeping myself involved in the ongoing service of cat rescue, work, classes, and writing, life was full and good.

At this same time, my mother and cousin went to visit a relative who had just bought a house on a lake. While there, they shared about my recent divorce, the pain I was going through, and suggested that the relative give me a call, as he had just gone through a divorce himself. A week later, the phone rang, and it was him. We had an enjoyable conversation, and he invited me out to his lake house for a bonfire that weekend. Feeling a strong hesitation, I thanked him but declined.

He called again the next week and asked me out again. This time I laid reservations aside and drove out for a visit. When he showed me his house, as I walked in, it was like coming home, and I instantly fell in love with this little cabin. It was cozy and warm and felt so right. I remember thinking, *I could live here*, before the thought passed as we went outside and the evening progressed. We continued to catch up on each other's lives, talking about our divorces and who did what and why. As I left for home, I reflected on the evening and thought it would be nice to visit now and then, before putting the whole thing out of my mind.

He was obviously not thinking the same thing, as he began to call on a regular basis. Our conversations mainly centered on him, his life, and what he had gone through. He began to unload during those calls, sharing his darkest secrets and fears, the wrongs he had done, and how he was searching for answers. It felt to me like he was looking for redemption and seeking peace, and it reminded me of myself. Listening with no judgment, as who was I to judge, I felt honored that he trusted me enough to share his deepest thoughts. It was here that he first became determined to keep me close. He had released his pain and had found someone strong enough to hold it for him. And in me, he had found strength, comfort, and peace. He wasn't about to let me go, even though he knew little about me, as he never asked, and I was still in the habit of keeping my voice silenced, so I never shared.

The calls continued, along with the invitations to come out to visit him once again. Occasionally, I would visit. We would go out for dinner or dancing at the local pubs and had many good times. But then things began to feel off kilter, as I sensed something else was on his mind. One evening, while we were out, he put his arm around my shoulders. Quietly, I told him I wasn't comfortable with this. But smiling, he left his arm in place. The feeling was one of entrapment, but I was not brave enough to again speak up or move away. With that weak resistance, he saw an open door, and the advances increased. Even though I felt like running, I seemed frozen in place.

In an effort to prevent this from happening again, I began to decline his invitations. This did not work. Visits to my home began. He would show up after he got out of work and would be waiting for me when I got home. Sometimes he wouldn't wait, but I knew he had been there, as he would leave thoughtful, touching cards or books that he thought I would like. There were many times he would show up on the weekends under the pretense that he had seen some repairs that needed to be done around my house. While I wasn't thrilled with this new development, I maintained my silence as I had always done. This went on for some time.

It was then that my mother started putting on the pressure. She saw a man with a good job, representing security; she liked him and was again worried about me, just wanting me to find a good man and settle down once and for all. To her, marriage was stability, safety, and security, and she made sure to let me know that this one I shouldn't let go. So, with pressure from him and pressure from her, I felt myself weaken. It seemed so much easier to just go with the flow than to fight my way upstream against the current I felt flowing against me and maintain my freedom. As always, in my attempt to please and not upset others, I was allowing the situation to progress where it would.

One weekend, he threw a big party at the lake, and I drove out with my brother. We both had a fun, exciting time—with boating, skiing, meeting many new people, and lots and lots of drinking. My brother decided it was late and time for him to leave. Seeing I was still enjoying myself, he left without me. When I noticed this, I had one of those strong uh-oh feelings inside.

Later in the night, after most everyone had left, the advances became insistent, and with me being who I thought I was at the time, I just submitted, and we had sex. This would intensify his insistent pursuit, and while I was nowhere ready to commit to anything or anyone, I made no effort to stop the momentum either.

After this, he started talking about me moving in with him. Even though I loved his little house and had finally made the decision to sell the house I'd never wanted to live in, I was not in love with him. Telling him no and why, I proceeded to put my house on the market and decided I would make my future plans when they were needed. This is never a good idea, as when the deadline comes and we are pressured to make a decision *now*, we are apt to make the wrong one. The pressure to move in with him became constant. And to my surprise, my mother supported this move. She had always wanted to keep me as close to her as possible and knew that, if I moved in with him, I would be an hour's drive away, so I was beyond surprised. Now, with this double-sided pressure, I began to consider it, even though the idea held no real excitement.

Finally, I told him I would make the move, and he was thrilled and excited. Selling or giving away most of my furniture and large items, we packed what was left, and I moved into his house.

As I walked through the door, I felt myself freeze as everything inside me began screaming, *No, no, no!* As I proceeded to put my belongings away, the anxiety continued to grow until it was like a heavy weight on my chest. I felt like a trapped animal desperately looking for a way to escape. Beyond any doubt, I knew I couldn't stay. Although feeling great fear, I finally found my voice and told him that I couldn't do this, that I wasn't ready, and I had to move back home. When I spoke those words, I felt a great peace, a feeling I was not going to give up.

Angrily, he began to try and talk me out of it, but I wouldn't budge and began to repack my belongings. Seeing this, he finally helped me load my car and his truck, and we drove the hour back to my house, where he helped me unpack and then left in a huff. Feeling nothing but great relief, I hoped that he was so angry he would never call or visit again.

My hope was not to be, as he didn't give up. And neither did my mother. The calls and visits continued, and it was clear that he was obsessed with having me. Over and over, I explained that all I wanted was friendship, and I maintained my distance emotionally, if not physically, as he was often there.

That was summer. By late fall, the bids began coming in on my home. I had a buyer with nowhere to move. The current was flowing swiftly, and I felt like I was drowning, with nothing in sight to cling to. We talked. He said he was willing to have me move in as his roommate and promised not to apply any pressure to make our relationship anything more. Reminding me that the two of us had had a lot of fun doing things together and meeting new people, he assured me that we could do this as friends. Taking him at his word, I agreed.

Later, I would look at this decision and see an emerging butterfly who'd wanted only to try her wings and fly free but had landed right in the middle of a spider's web, one that would entangle her for many years to come. She hadn't been seriously looking at where she was going, with no idea where she wanted to be and had ignored all the many warnings signs along her way.

This was a very strange experience for me. While he wanted one thing, he was skillful enough to let things proceed as they were, as he knew I had just enough resistance to say no. This only encouraged him to finally win. While living there, I continued to take classes at the bookstore and would come home to share my experiences with him. He would listen, and his listening thrilled me, as it was so new. It was so refreshing to have someone interested in what I was saying that it worked in me like an aphrodisiac. He soon learned that listening to me earned him what he had been waiting for all along—a sexual union binding us closer together.

Still, even though our relationship had progressed into the physical, I continued to fluctuate between wanting to stay and wanting to run. And in seeing this, he proposed marriage, as he was taking no chances. So we married, as I was tired of resisting.

Years later, my husband shared with me that he saw me as the trophy wife he was determined to have. Beautiful, slim, and willowy; fun and exciting; kind to all and accepting of everyone I met, I was the woman all the men around us wanted for their own, and he was determined to have me for himself, to adorn his arm. Not seeing this for myself, lost in a self-image that was like nothing he was seeing, I was easily led.

As for me, I was beginning to see in him safety and security. And encouraged by my mother, who wanted me finally settled and secure, I had accepted what he offered. Each with our own agenda of what it was we wanted to take from the other, we started our life together with no goal other than to take what it was we wanted at the time. With no shared goals, dreams, wants, or desires, this would eventually lead to disaster when what it was we'd married to get was no longer enough.

This was a difficult chapter to review, as it was here that I saw an inner guidance that was trying to help me avoid an experience that was within my power to step away from. The emotions I was feeling—the anxiety, the many feelings of hesitation, and the extreme discomfort—were all my heart's voice trying to show me that I was entering into a relationship for all the wrong reasons once again. Bringing thoughts of the past, with a self-image based on the past, into the present is no place to begin a future. At that time, this was where both of us were at, lost in the past and trying to redeem ourselves in the present with no thought of the future.

More was asking to be seen here. In my unwillingness to enter fully into the pain that was calling to me after my second divorce, I had missed the lessons pain was trying to reveal to me. Not being learned, these lessons would be repeated until they were finally learned and not until then. It was so clear now, but it hadn't been then. Pain was a voice calling to me to look, trying to show me where I had separated myself from my inner voice, deafened by the thoughts I was choosing to think. If I had followed pain where it was trying to lead me at that time, it would have led me to a better understanding of myself and to peace.

No longer would I resist pain, try to run away from it, or try to explain it away. Rather, I would listen and follow it where it was leading me, as it would lead me to truth. Now that I knew, it was from a place of knowing I would move forward, a bit signed, but alive, to see what else I'd missed then but needed to know now.

Chapter 11

I CAN'T BREATHE! WHOSE HAND IS OVER MY MOUTH NOW?!

*O' what a tangled web we weave when
first we practice to deceive.*

—Walter Scott

$\mathcal{I}$n the beginning, it was just the two of us. We settled into a routine, going out often; visiting a few neighbors; and, in general, enjoying each other's company. My sister died in our first couple of years together, and I had watched as her long-held fear of dying of cancer wrapped itself around her so tightly that it squeezed the very breath from her body. While I was sad for her and her family, I also felt a sense of relief, as she had been the biggest judge of my life. Throughout this experience, my husband was kind, gentle, and caring, and this brought us closer together for a while.

It was shortly after this that his attitude began to shift. Perhaps it had been shifting long before and I just hadn't recognized it. Slowly, the attempts to control began, along with the game of guilt, and I had the sudden realization that I had married my mother.

While I recognized this at the time, I still did not see that I had been drawn to this relationship because it was familiar; and I knew how to act—how to hide myself and be what and who another wanted me to be. Bringing the past into the present, I was like a moth led to the flame, where my wings were about to be singed again.

As the criticism intensified, both of what I did and didn't do, he began to focus on finances. We had a joint account. Both of us were making good money, and my goal was to save, pay extra on the house loan, and eventually be debt free, as my desire was to travel. He disagreed, as his belief was that money was to be enjoyed in the moment, and he had no desire to travel. Of course, desires, beliefs, or dreams were not something we had ever discussed before our marriage, so we'd started out heading in two different directions from the beginning. The battle continued. Surrounded by his criticism, I began to sink into the familiar guilt that had controlled me all of my life, losing sight of my dreams and desires again. It seemed easier just to let go and follow the dreams and desires of another.

Feeling miserable, I found myself somewhere I did not want to be, with no idea what to do about it. Remembering the astrology readings offered at the bookstore I used to frequent, I booked an appointment. This was something I had never done, as I did not care for the idea of someone else putting his or her ideas into my mind. But I thought, just maybe, I might find the answer I was seeking.

At the reading, I was told that the reader had never seen such an amazing and powerful chart. Excited, she began to ask me about all the talents I must have, as my chart showed I was very gifted and creative. To all of her questions about music, art, and crafts, I could only respond with a feeble no. Finally, I told her that I loved to write. She waved her hand as if to wave the answer off as insignificant, and here the reading ended. Not only did I leave without an answer, but I left depleted, defeated, and believing I had wasted all these gifts and had nothing to offer anyone, never thinking to look on the fact that I had amazing potential. In despair, I returned home to have my worthlessness reinforced once again. I could do nothing right.

Every week, I visited my mother an hour away, joining her for dinner and spending a couple of hours conversing and catching up. It was especially important at this time, as she had just been diagnosed with the possibility of cancer and was undergoing chemotherapy. One night, I unloaded, sharing all the criticism and complaints I was hearing at home. When I paused, she quietly asked me why I was putting up with all of this. In shock, I just stared at her, as it had never occurred to me that I did not have to put up with it! All of my life, she had taught me that I had to put up with what I was given, and I had unknowingly sunk into the belief that I was to take whatever someone gave, and I had no choice. To hear her say this, after all of these years, I was beyond shocked. My whole belief system was shaken. As I sat there, she continued laying out the plan in my mind of when and how to leave.

With my thoughts swirling on the way home—weighing pros and cons, what-ifs and ramifications—I returned home undecided. That is until I walked through the door to more criticism. In that moment, I made up my mind to leave.

The next morning, I called my mother to let her know that I had made the decision to move in with her and then made arrangements for the move the next day. Feeling that I had to share this decision with my husband, I called him from work and suggested we meet after work at a local pub for dinner, as it was a safe, neutral place. That night, we ate and made small talk, and he again criticized something I had said or done. Gathering my courage, I looked at him and told him my decision and that I would be leaving the next day. He looked at me, first with shock and then with scorn. He didn't believe I would.

The next morning, he left for work, and I busily began to pack what I had brought with me. It didn't take long. By the time my brother arrived, I was ready and anxious to leave. It took a short amount of time to load his truck, and we were on our way. As I drove up the hill leading to the main road, I stopped; looked around me at what I was leaving; and said out loud, "I do not miss you," and drove away.

That night, my husband called. He was in a state of disbelief and began berating me for leaving. Calmly, I informed him I didn't have to listen, and with steely resolve, I hung up. I was *free*!

He called again the next day, only this time with tears and remorse, begging me to come home. With the same strength, I reminded him of his treatment, his criticizing, judgmental words and bluntly told him he must be joking. Feeling stronger than I had felt in many years, I believed that, for once, I had made a decision for me instead of for someone else.

This began a daily litany of calls, sometimes two or three times a day. He began sharing with me thoughts, feelings, actions I was unaware of. And in listening, I asked myself if he was cleansing or manipulating, trying to grasp his purpose. Finally, deciding he was being honest with me and that he trusted me enough to be honest, I felt no judgment. But his honesty did not move me to return.

Finally gone, I felt a semblance of peace in working and caring for my mother, but I found my evenings were difficult. Soon, I began driving after work to the old local cemetery where my father was buried. There, on the isolated two-track, I would sit and record my thoughts and feelings. Next to where I parked was an ancient, gnarled pine, and I began to talk with it, sharing my thoughts and my heart while it listened. Sensing an ancient wisdom and strength emanating from it, I named it Olaf, the ancient one, and we would have in-depth conversations. I rarely wanted to leave the peace I found there. Although I was also parked next to my father's grave, I made no attempt to talk with him. We had not talked when he was alive, so I held no hope of talking with him now; and if he was listening, he made no comment.

The calls from my husband continued, turning into pleasant, newsy conversations, full of concern for how I was and what I was doing. And I began to relax into the conversations, as communication was what I had wanted all along. Plus, I was growing lonely. Work and caring for my mother with no real social life was growing boring. My husband stayed away for the first three months but eventually began coming over, on the pretense of helping me and my mother with yard work, repairs, and visits with her to inquire into how she was doing. When he would come over, he always brought beautiful, poetic, thoughtful cards; books that he knew I liked; or artwork he knew I had been wanting. He exerted no pressure for me to return but was slowly wooing, luring me back.

He called one evening, asking me to rejoin the bowling league we had been members of, saying that I was missed, and the team would like to have me back. After several such invitations, I finally agreed. When I shared this with my mother, her face grew concerned, and she told me I was making a mistake. But I was no longer sure I could trust her, as I had begun to sense that she had a plan for me all her own; she enjoyed having me there, and her plan all along was for the two of us to be together forever. Sensing this trap, I began to feel like I had escaped one spider's web only to have another being woven around me.

Still, with no concrete plan of my own, I began joining my husband one night a week on our league and found that I was enjoying his company and having fun again. We were back at the beginning of our relationship once again, with him showing me love and respect and listening to my thoughts and us simply having a good time together. After another month, I moved back in with him.

My mother's face as I packed and moved away was full of sorrow. While I wished happiness for her, I could not, would not fulfill her dream. So I returned to continue the dance my husband and I had begun, each hearing a different melody, as so many in relationships do—dancing alone, giving each a taste of what the other wants, but never fully giving in or giving all. We each had our own agenda, with neither of us knowing how to express the needs and desires within us. The dance would continue until one or both of us became so tired and exhausted we would just stop the dance to rest. We were not there yet, not truly knowing what it was we were dancing to or how to achieve a state of union within it.

A truth stuck out boldly while I was remembering this portion of my past, as I recognized that I had placed myself in the same situation I had been in when I was young. Once again, I was that little child with a voice no one wanted to hear. What a tangled web I myself had woven with my own deceptive thoughts from the past about who I was and what I deserved to have in my life. In always projecting the blame onto others, I had been missing the vital truth that I had been doing all the weaving myself with the thoughts I had chosen to think, about myself, about others, about marriage, and about life itself. No one had deceived me more than I had been deceiving myself, but I had been too busy pushing the responsibility unto others, too afraid to look at what I was doing by dragging the past along with me. Blaming my husband for a lack of honest, open communication was easier than recognizing that I had no honest, open communication with him or with myself or even about myself and was choosing instead to live within the deception of blame. Still seeing myself as a victim with no voice, I had been weaving quite the tangled web all along.

It was during this review that I was shown a three-legged race. It takes two people working together as one to win the race. Communication is the first step, joining minds to have one successful plan. With no communication, there is no plan, and when the race starts, each steps out with the wrong foot, and both end up in a tangled heap to never reach the finish line. This was the story of our marriage. Each of us was blaming the other, neither of us was talking or even knowing how or where to begin; and there we were in a tangled heap.

The picture wasn't pretty, but it was very revealing. So it was time to take these gifts of truth with me and leave this chapter to find out what else life had been trying to show me now that I was willing to look. Finally I was ready to leave this sticky mess I'd been weaving and to be free to obtain what life had to offer when I gave up my ways for a new way.

Chapter 12

IT IS EASIER TO GET FORGIVEN THAN TO GET PERMISSION: THINK WRONG? THINK AGAIN!

*The winds of storm tear away all we do
not need to show us who we are.*

—Arthur Golden

Once I returned home, we were both on our best behavior and returned to our routine of work, going out, and talking. But our talks were guarded, with me not wanting to draw any form of criticism or rock the boat and him wanting to keep me close, fearing I would leave again. Trust was gone, but neither of us realized this at the time. It was just comfortable enough for us to spend time together and enjoy the life we were making.

My husband had many creeds he lived by and loved to quote on a regular basis to whoever was around to hear—and even to those who had heard them time and again. One of his favorites was, "It is easier to get forgiven than it is to get permission." And he lived by this creed. Those words spoke to me of lies and deception, instilling an even deeper distrust, and I would ask myself, *Just what is he thinking about doing that he would even need forgiveness for?* Much, I would soon find out, as the storms of change were brewing.

First, my husband decided to try his hand at rentals. Two small houses came up for sale near us, and at the price they were asking, it appeared to be a win-win. Thinking this could possibly lead to my dream of financial independence, I agreed to give it a try, although I suggested we first talk with someone who was experienced who could give us advice and tips on being successful. This idea was squashed, as he believed he could do it all on his own. And as always, I kept silent, never to bring it up again, but it was never far from my thoughts. We bought the houses and began renting them out and, through this venture, we began meeting new people who eventually became good friends and, although our renters would come and go, they always came back to visit.

Shortly after this, I decided to quit my long-distance job, as the commute was expensive and exhausting. He was all for this, as he had never cared for me having a life outside of his realm and wanted me close to home. Settling in at home, I took over the yard work and landscaping and handled the rentals while he worked. Eventually becoming bored, I started my own business as a representative for a well-known company. Through this venue, I met more people in the neighborhood, and our circle of friends began rapidly growing. We lived on a lake and owned a large pole barn with an upstairs equipped for fun and company. A new life was beginning. My husband built a huge covered bonfire pit in the middle yard, and our home soon became the local party place, drawing in more people, as friends invited friends, all of whom began stopping by often.

Eventually, people were gathered at our place every evening and weekend, and this would become our new norm. Being constantly surrounded by people, it was during this time that he and I began to drift further apart, as we had no time to talk, we were rarely ever alone, and communication became totally null and void. With people always there and because both of us found it fun at the time, we quit going out on our own together anywhere, ever, because we might miss someone who showed up while we were gone. We were both becoming quite content with this life, with neither of us seeing where we were headed.

Changes continued to occur, and with a growing sense of dissatisfaction, I sought and found another job close by, instantly falling in love with the work and the people I worked with and quickly going from part time to full time. Here I was happy; here I was fulfilled; here I was seen, recognized, and acknowledged for my contributions in serving. My husband was not as happy, as I was again finding a life outside of home, and the push and pull would begin with him criticizing my work and me wanting to be there more than at home. Another wedge had come between us, with neither of us recognizing it was even there. At the same time, I was still handling all the responsibilities at home, building my business, and partying—keeping myself busy and allowing no time to think beyond what was in front of me.

More changes were to come and sooner than I expected. With life full to overflowing, my husband suddenly told me that he was tired of our little home and wanted a bigger, nicer house in its place and already had plans to tear down what we had and rebuild. Panicking, as I loved our little home, I tried to change his mind. But my words fell on deaf ears. He had made up his mind and had called a contractor. Listening as the contractor gave a bid for the design and rebuilding, I found the cost astronomical, but my husband only saw that we could well afford the cost.

With what had always been my way, I eventually agreed, asking myself silently, *Is this going to kill me?*

This would become an ongoing dialogue I would have with myself in the years to come, not realizing that the accumulation of pain and resentment causing me to ask this question was already growing and would eventually kill us in the end if allowed to continue. Moving into one of our rentals, we signed on the dotted line, and construction began. With a heavy heart, I watched as my special little home was destroyed to build a house that I would never call my own. He had gotten what he wanted, didn't believe he needed my permission, and fully expected to be forgiven. He did not realize that he was pushing us further and further apart, as I began to believe that my happiness meant nothing to him.

The winds of change were still brewing around us, as my husband—now eligible for a full retirement pension—began talking about retiring. Reminding him of the huge debt load we had just assumed, I showed him the numbers to let him know that now was not the time to cut his income in half and asked him to wait one more year until we were more financially stable. To my surprise and appreciation, he appeared to listen and agreed, promising to wait one more year. I thanked him profusely, greatly relieved.

A few months after this promise, I came home from work to find him leaning against his truck, arms crossed, waiting for me to get home. A sudden sense of dread rose within and I knew something was up, something that I was not going to like. As I approached him, he looked at me with a sneer and bluntly informed me he had put in his retirement papers that day, and he would be done within the month. My heart felt like it stopped, and I couldn't breathe. The disbelief at his betrayal and deceit knocked the air out of me, and I couldn't speak. With the same sneer, he told me that he could do all of this himself, that he didn't need me to do what he wanted to do, and that he would do it all with or without me!

In that moment, I hated him with a hatred I didn't know I could feel. Every fiber of my body was filled with hate, and in the intensity of this feeling, I couldn't say a word. Not wanting to look at him a minute longer, I walked away on shaking legs. For days afterward, I couldn't look at him or speak. My thoughts were racing with what to do and what not to do—to leave or to stay, to cry or to rage.

And I did nothing. With my thoughts totally consumed with the deceit and the lies, the thought of leaving now, with all of this new debt between us, seemed impossible. I totally pushed it out of my mind, weakly telling myself that this would not kill me. Frozen in time, I continued to go to work and come home to find him drunk and happy in his retirement, welcoming me home. He was sure he had won and would be forgiven as, after all, I was still there, wasn't I?!

As my distrust and resentment grew, the chasm between us widened, and never once did we talk about any of it. Still alive physically, we were emotionally dead. And as the parties continued, the friends remained and multiplied. I distanced myself as much as possible in the activity around us with whoever or whatever was available. By now, I had totally forsaken my writing and had not picked up a book to absorb in years. A heavy sorrow was growing in my heart. And I allowed myself no time to wonder why or where this was coming from.

One day, I found myself driving down the highway at seventy-five miles an hour and had the thought, *I can pull out in front of this oncoming semitruck and end it all, just get out of here.* This thought came not just once but several times, and it was strong. In the midst of this thought, something always called me back, distracted my thoughts, and I would drive on. But, the sorrow lingered, was always there, even in the midst of this seemingly happy party place I was calling home.

Was this life going to kill me? Oh, yes ... it already was. Within, I was withering and dying, like a morning glory bloom on the vine during a draught, only I didn't know then what I was thirsting for.

In reliving this period of my story, I was shocked at the intensity of the feelings that remained after all this time, as the pain still felt so real all these years later. Unable to go on, all I could do was ask for help to see what I needed to see in this remembered pain. It was slow in coming, as focusing on pain is like a thick blanket that hides the truth from being seen. But I struggled to see beyond the suffocating feeling to what this pain was trying to teach me.

Very slowly, I began to see another picture, and this one was the truth of what I had been doing to myself—again, still. It was with total shock that I realized what a victim I saw myself as being, completely believing that I had no choice, no voice, and no right to make any decision—that I could only accept the one handed to me and had ended up in a living hell of my own making.

Shaking my head, I asked myself, "Why couldn't I see then what I see now?" The answer was simple. My own self-image, the one I had made, had stood in my way, blocking me from seeing anything but who I had made by my thoughts from the past.

Once again, an image appeared of my mother, the one who silently gave up her dreams and hopes, only to blame and fall into a deep, dark pit of resentment in which she lived until the day she died. This was the woman I did not want to be, had sworn I would never be; yet here I saw myself once again walking in her very shoes.

As healing continued its work within me, I began to take back some of the resentment and the blame that I had laid upon my husband, beginning to clearly see that I had been hurting myself all along. He had only done what he was given permission to do by my own silence. We'd never had open, honest communication; how would he know my hopes and dreams when I never told him or ever made one effort to stand up and just say no to what he wanted? He couldn't know that he was leading me somewhere I didn't want to be, because I never spoke, never shared, never stood strong for what I wanted, which might have gained his respect and brought us closer together to share a common goal. Long ago, I had made the decision to hide the voice I had been given, because I was afraid of the pain of criticism and judgment, only to bring pain with me in this moment by my silence. No, I had not seen this then, but I was seeing it now.

Sitting with this memory and reviewing all I had been shown took time, as I found myself resisting what I needed to see, not wanting to own the part I'd played in causing my own pain. When the weed of a belief has been allowed to grow, its roots are long, and it takes continued, steady effort to pull it up so that it can be removed. This was happening to me now. While it felt like my heart was being torn, I began to understand that this was a temporary pain of a lie being torn away, a lie that I no longer wanted in my life, so that truth can be planted. With new insight now in place, I could move further out of the darkness and into a space of light. It was time to move on. I was only halfway through this self-revealing story of wrong thinking. Finally, I was ready.

Chapter 13

THIS MOUNTAIN IS *HIGH!* ISN'T THERE AN EASIER WAY?

Over every mountain there is a path, although
it may not be seen from the valley.

—Theodore Roethke

*F*eeling like I'd been climbing a mountain and trying to get out of the valley of despair, I was tired, exhausted, and wanted a break. But it was not to be, for more changes were headed our way, and they would happen in rapid succession. They would be dark, painful experiences that would tear the remaining shaky foundation out from under us.

First came the betrayal of a trusted friend, resulting in the loss of many we had called friends, as each one wanted to escape the turmoil this betrayal had caused. Next came a fire that consumed our barn, holding antique vehicles and furniture, old family pictures and memorabilia from the past. More than all that, it would consume years of happy, fun memories, precious to us both, like the slate was being wiped clean. Soon after this occurred, one of our rental tenants was busted for manufacturing and selling meth, resulting in the ridicule of neighbors, the condemnation of the rental, and many months of cleaning and testing that cost thousands of dollars. My husband began sinking into a bitter depression that I, wrapped up in my own grief and loss (and, as I would later discover, blame), didn't see at the time.

Just as I was thinking that this dark cloud had passed, one more storm was about to hit. My husband had previously started his own business, buying the needed equipment and storing it in our barn. A vindictive neighbor called the county to report that my husband was unlawfully operating a business on our property, and the county came down on him hard. Although the allegation was not true and could have been easily overturned, he had no fight left. He gave up and sold his equipment, losing every activity that had once given him purpose, and sank further into darkness, spending his time alone in the solitary dark new barn, recently built but holding no meaning for him. He was alone in his grief; darkness had descended; and he saw no light, lost in his dark thoughts. Although I felt I had little light to offer, having my own dark thoughts, I would go out to visit with him, where I was met with either stony silence or anger, and I would soon leave.

Throughout all of this, I had my job, and it helped save my sanity. It was one place where I could go and feel accepted, honored for the work I was doing, and surrounded by people who liked and acknowledged me—none of which I was receiving at home. My husband, now with nothing to do, no place to go, and few friends left, sat alone day after day in his dark barn with his increasingly dark thoughts of blame and pain.

After several months, I came home to have him waiting for me. He told me that he had to get away, that he wanted to go to a warmer climate over the winter, and that I was to quit my job and make the arrangements. In disbelief, I looked at him and simply said no. Having lost enough, I would not, could not lose what had kept my sanity for so long and walk away to follow him again. The sense of panic turned to strength, and I asked him if he truly thought I would want to go somewhere to be alone with him after all the years of anger, disregard, and disrespect. No, I was not willing to make another sacrifice to lose again. This began what would become years of bitter, angry outbursts, him blaming me for his misery, believing that, if he bullied long enough, I would give in. And why wouldn't I? I always had, and he believed I would again. Yes, I'd trained him well.

Struggling throughout to talk rationally with him and trying to compromise, I suggested we go somewhere warm for a couple of weeks and scope out the area to see if we could find a place to winter over, instead of just abruptly leaving. In the back of my mind was the hope that a couple of weeks away might change the track of destruction we were on. My words fell on deaf ears, as it was to be his way or no way. Nothing I said was of any value to him. He began talking over me, interrupting, or angrily walking away. In this environment, we continued to live together, both miserable and unable to talk.

In the middle of this turmoil, a friend showed up at our door late at night, an older man in his late seventies we had known for years. He was homeless, through unforeseen circumstances, and arrived at our door with only the clothes he had on. The next day, we moved our friend into our remaining rental, where he would live for three years, growing happier and stronger day by day and spending his time in the barn with my husband, and he soon became my buffer. Yet, toward the end, he too began to take the brunt of my husband's obsessive anger.

One day after not having seen our friend for several days, I went next door to ask him if he needed anything. Walking in, I found him lying dead on the floor. My heart stopped as I stared before checking his pulse and leaving to call 9-1-1. My husband was out in his usual place, the dark barn, and I called him on the local to tell him what had happened and that the police would soon arrive. Instead of coming down to assist, he asked if there was anything he could do. And I sarcastically laughed, telling him it had all been taken care of, inwardly blaming him for the death of our friend, as he had never checked on him as I had asked.

My husband never came down to check on me until well after the police had arrived and I had taken care of arrangements. Later, after all had been taken care of, I went out to the barn, shaken, traumatized, and still in disbelief, to find him sitting there with a couple of nearby friends who had heard the sirens. Not one of them asked me how I was doing and acted as if nothing had happened. While it hurt, it gave me a resolve to get away—far, far away. *If I'm going to be alone, with no one who cares about me and no one to talk with, I might as well live alone.* Again, it was just a thought, and I took no action, although the thought began to take root.

As a year stretched into two and then into three, I began to realize that, in his depression and my own struggle to hold onto what was left, our relationship was basically dead. We both knew it but never talked about it. But for some reason, I still held onto hope, and in a final attempt to salvage what we could, I asked him to seek help. Surprisingly, he did. His doctor sent him to talk with a therapist, who asked him only if he cried a lot or had thoughts of suicide. His truthful answer was no, and he did not share the intense anger he was living in, so the therapist sent him out, telling him he was not depressed and needed no help.

Being told there was nothing wrong with him, my husband continued to blame and carry the load of hateful, painful thoughts within him, striking out at everyone in his grief. Any attempts on my part to help him talk through all that had happened, to get his thoughts out in the open in order to clearly look at and deal with them, were met with anger; he would often tell me to shut up or simply walk out the door. Clearly, I was not the one to help, as I had become the enemy that was tearing his life apart. It was here that I withdrew in an attempt to salvage what little self-worth I felt I had left.

This began what I call my hibernation period. I withdrew into my small office in the house, and it soon became my haven, where I would slink away to hide and lick my wounds. In quiet desperation, it was here that I began to make an attempt to figure out how I had ended up in this dark, negative place I was now in. By now, I was beginning to realize that I could not blame everyone in my life and that there was something that I was doing or not doing that had brought me here.

So, I again began to write, logging my every thought, emotion, fear, hope, and dream and asking out loud again and again what I was doing to myself and why! Never had I felt so alone, but it was here that I would soon discover I was not alone, nor had I ever been, only in my own thoughts. My questions were about to be answered, as I was now cracked open enough to begin to hear something other than my own roller-coaster thoughts that were always racing, only to end up at the same destination.

It was here in the silence that I began to hear a Voice. Not audible, but clearly not my own swirling thoughts, as this Voice had a peace and strength that was like nothing I had ever heard, and it resonated in my heart. Hungry for more, I listened. Slowly, layer upon layer was revealed, and I found myself at the bottom of all this muck and mire that had buried me all of my life. It was here at the bottom that I began to sense another, someone I hadn't seen before and who was just waiting to be looked for and known.

Within these many layers, I would soon be shown how I had kept so many parts of me separated—my birth, my childhood, my teenage experiences when I was desperately searching for my identity, and the loss of church and husbands as I stumbled in the dark. Feeling guilt and pain, I had turned my back on the memories, refusing to look at the truth they held, further separating myself from my true self within my own self-judgment and condemnation. Yet, I now knew that I *had* to look, to acknowledge, as I had been carrying this heavy load of despair and pain with me everywhere I went. It was here that I began to understand that I would never be whole if I kept any aspect of myself, or my journey, separate and alone.

With help, I began learning how to look back and laugh and cry within each one of my experiences, to feel the pain, and to finally understand my search for love and acceptance and attempt to join us all together as one. This looking back at what had been was to be the start of true healing and a new beginning.

In the meantime, I would occasionally venture out to my husband's dark, solitary hideaway and try to simply socialize, to be present, and perhaps to talk about where we were and where we were going. Yet, time and again, I was met with a jealous, angry onslaught of criticism and verbal abuse. Pure disregard or disinterest I could have accepted and lived with. The abuse, I would not.

Unknowingly, I was growing in confidence and self-respect, seeing myself in a new way, with new choices. So, I would return to my solitude and continue to write and to listen. There were times that I would still cry out for help, as I would find myself lost in my own self-flagellation, fighting off guilt in seeing what I had been doing to myself. Then, once again, I would hear that I was still too busy trying to climb out of this valley of despair all by myself, momentarily forgetting the strength and clear direction that was now available to me.

Relaxing, I began to realize that if I had not gone through all that I had been through the last few years, I might not have withdrawn from the world's draw long enough to find myself. This new and different thought would change my vision of what was to transpire ahead. In the quiet, I would continue to search, to write, and to listen.

Yes, the mountain was still there, but now I knew that I had to get out of my own way and allow myself to be led by One who knew an easier way and had the strength and wisdom to help me get to where I needed to be, which was out of the valley and on top of the mountain. Beginning to see the whole picture, I could see that every decision I had ever made, and every decision I had allowed others to make for me, were all based on how I saw myself at the time. Now, I was beginning to look for my true self and knew that I could change the picture I had been seeing all my life!

The mountain that I alone had made with my own thoughts was a tall one, and it was going to be a steep climb. But now I knew that I could make it and that I would reach the top. From this viewpoint, I would have a clear view of where I had been and the rough, rocky path I had chosen by inwardly fighting for my life and my right to be, fighting against everything and everyone that came my way. The good, the bad and the ugly, I had fought it all. Here at the top, I would see that, yes, there was an easier way, and it wasn't the way I had been choosing. Past ready for peace, something I had been seeking for so many years, I could feel it coming, slowly building within me, and ready to explode into my reality.

Placing my hand in my newfound Friend's, I was ready to move on. There was more to see, and I now knew that the sights would be unlike anything I had ever seen, where beautiful life would be blooming, replacing the strangling weeds that had been slowly squeezing the life out of me. Yes, I was now excited and ready for what might lie ahead. There would be a lot, but I was not going there alone any longer.

Chapter 14

OH SIGH ... WHAT NOW?!

We do not see things as they are, we see them as we are.

—Anais Nin

*I*n the midst of all this emotional upheaval, there was another story that needed to be completed. It was the story about my relationship with my mother. It was to be challenge, as our lifelong relationship had been a challenge. Not really ready for it, as I felt a bit overwhelmed with what was on my plate already, I found, once again, I didn't get to choose.

After I left her home and returned to live with my husband, my mother continued living alone, burying herself deeper and deeper into resentment, cutting off old friends, shunning those who attempted to reach out to her, staying home, and waiting for me or my brother to visit. We were all she wanted and all she was determined to have. Using guilt to guide and direct us, we both visited her weekly, having lunch or dinner and making small talk to fill her long hours alone. Often, remarks were made to let us know that we were failing her, had failed her in the past, and were continuing to fail her now by living our own lives, while she was left alone. We merely listened ... and soaked up the guilt.

For years my brother had wanted to travel, as from a young boy he had wanted to see the world. Although now retired and having bought a motor home to travel in, he experienced guilt that would not allow him to leave and fulfill his long-held desire. He wistfully talked about it often, but we both knew it was never going to happen while our mother was still with us. I, too, enjoyed traveling but would keep my trips short, so that I was not gone too long. Even this did not appease her, as I was met with stony silence when I returned. Both my brother and I just lived with it.

One day, I got a phone call from my mother and found this very strange, as she never called anyone, waiting for others to call her and resenting us when we did not. Concerned, I asked her if she was okay, not expecting her next words. Speaking firmly and sharply, she informed me that she no longer wanted to cook and clean, was done with household maintenance, and wanted to sell her house and move into an assisted living home. She had elected me to search and to find a home of her liking, and my brother and I would make the arrangements to move her there. When I asked when she wanted to move, her answer was a quick, sharp *now!*

To say I was blown away by her orders is an understatement, and my thoughts were swirling as my vision of this independent, strong mother came crashing down all around me. I believed that she had given up; that she was ready for the end; and that, somehow, it was all my fault. As I hung up, I began to cry, and sobbing was where my husband found me minutes later. Holding me, he asked me what was wrong. I told him what my mother had said and my thoughts about her words. As I shared my fear-filled thoughts, he tried to assure me that it was not as it appeared. She just wanted to be cared for, as she had cared for others all of her life. His words were reassuring.

Feeling somewhat optimistic, I began the search to find her what she was looking for. Hours of calling, visiting homes, sharing with her what I had found, and setting up appointments for her to visit and make the final decision took months. Looking back, I saw that she, once again, had me where she wanted me—with my total focus on her. My brother was also drawn in, as he would take her to visit the homes I had found. And she now had what she had what she been wanting all along—our total and complete attention.

Finally, she settled on a home, which was halfway between where my brother lived and where I was living, and then arrangements were made to move her and the few belongings she was allowed to take with her. Once she was settled, we thought she would be happy, as she had gotten what she wanted. But she wasn't.

She'd purposely chosen a place halfway between the two of us, so that we would visit her more often, totally discounting that we both had lives of our own, lives that were already full. My brother and I split our visits, so that both of us visited her twice a week.

We hoped that she would make friends with the other five women who were living with her, who often invited her out to the large sitting room, where they would knit, crochet, watch television, and talk. She refused, choosing instead to remain alone in her room, waiting for one of us and all the while thinking bitter thoughts about her life and how she was being treated.

When we would visit, she would sit with crossed arms and pinched lips, refusing to talk. After a while, when I would visit, I would first talk with the owners, two wonderful women who I thoroughly enjoyed visiting with. They would update me on how she was doing, the flower garden they had prepared outside her window to work in, and the bird feeder they had hung outside her window to enjoy, as I had told them she enjoyed both. When I would enter her room, I was met with an angry glare, as I had spent too much time talking with them and not with her. Talking rapidly and hoping to break the tension, I would ask her how her flower garden was going, what birds she was seeing, and what had she learned about the friendly women she was living with. These inquiries were met with a stony glare and complete silence. Our visits were not pleasant, and my brother was experiencing the same.

When my mother had first called me to tell me what she'd decided, I'd been thrown into great fear. At that time in my life, I was still so unknowingly wrapped within the web of guilt she had weaved so well that the thought of losing her made me feel that I would die if something happened to her. As time went on, I would find this web loosening more and more, as our time together became more and more unpleasant. And instead of drawing me tighter into her web, she was literally pushing me out of it.

There would be many more experiences to be had, because as time went on, she began developing imaginary illnesses; having attacks; and making numerous trips to the emergency room, where we were expected to rush to her side. This led to requiring more doctor visits than I can recall. For years it felt that I was spending more time in the hospital or in doctors' offices than I was at home.

Finally, my brother and I realized that this was another ploy to gain our full attention and focus only on her, so we quit running to the hospital every time the phone rang. Time after time, nothing was ever found to be physically wrong with her.

When she finally passed away at age eighty-nine, many years after she had moved, I felt nothing but great relief. She, herself, had cut the web she had woven around me, and there was no grief, only a sense of release.

In years to come, I would find that I was always eased slowly into an emotional preparedness where I could handle whatever came my way. My brother and I became very close after our mother passed, as it was just the two of us left in our family. Our father and sister had died years before. Now mom was gone, and our bond became tight. With him, too, I felt that I could not survive if he left me, for I believed I would be left all alone.

Yet I was to find that I would, I could survive, because, as my brother aged, he also became bitter, angry, and full of blame; his words were sharp and meant to cut. After years of being his caregiver, taking him to numerous doctor visits, sitting in the hospital during multiple surgeries, and visiting him at home several times a week, I was finally ready when he passed away, as well. It seemed like this was all meant to be, giving and giving and all the while being pushed further and further away until I could watch from a distance as they went on their way one by one. There was no grief, except for the grief of what they had done to their own lives—lives that could have been fulfilling and happy, if they had just allowed their thoughts to focus on all they had instead of focusing on what they thought they lacked.

This was a very valuable lesson and one I learned well, carrying this knowledge with me today. Not only did I learn to be thankful for all that I have been given, keeping my thoughts focused on the abundance in my life to share, I learned to be grateful for the knowledge that I would always be prepared ahead of time; when the time came for the departure of whatever had to depart from my life, I would be ready, having been given the foresight and strength to make it through.

At the end of this experience, I would also see that my mother had done the best she could with what she knew based on her own beliefs and judgments. She was ignorant to the truth of who I am, and her words and actions were not based on malicious intent to harm or maim. Rather, she aimed to form and protect, to mold and shape me into her own image, as this was all she knew. Can there be any blame for ignorance? I think not. This opened up my eyes to love. She was my earthly mother, who loved me the best she could. And for that, she would rest in peace within my heart.

But there, at the time that all this was occurring, I was still not at this place of peace. While the one who molded and shaped me to fit her image was now gone, her words were only out of my ears, not out of my head, where they still rang loudly. It would be much later that I would come to know and understand that she loved me with her whole being and, wanting to keep me safe, had instilled great fear within me. While I knew within me that the image she had painted in my thoughts was not true, it would take years to paint over this image and to paint my own of who I truly am.

With paintbrush in hand, it was time to pick up where I left off to discover more truth about who and what I truly am in order to revise the image I had allowed others to make.

Chapter 15

OMG! I MET SOMEONE AND FELL IN LOVE!

And the day came when the desire to
remain tight in the bud was more painful
than the risk it took to bloom.

—Anais Nin

With all I'd been shown, I found myself in dark despair—again ... still. What *was* I doing?! What had I *done* to be here?! Where in the hell was I going?! I was confused, miserable, and in pain, and I didn't want to be here any longer! Withdrawing even more and continuing to write and search, I now knew I had to find myself to go on, as I had no idea who I was or what I was doing, and I sure had no clue where I was going. As I wrote, I began to realize that I never had. Putting one foot in front of the other, I'd just moved forward, following any path others had set before me until it came to a dead end, where I would wait until someone led me to another path, which I would blindly follow. Why had I done this? What drove me down all these dead-end paths?! This was what I began searching for, and I knew that the answer was inside of me.

The hours in solitude grew longer as I searched, and very slowly, all the jumbled pieces of my life began to fall into place. Like a complex puzzle coming together, a picture began to form before my eyes. At the time, I was not looking for enlightenment (not even knowing what it was) but to find a way out of this misery and pain I was experiencing and to find some peace. Praying for peace, begging for peace, and repeating all the right affirmations that were supposed to bring peace, I still felt nothing but emptiness and such deep sadness.

It was here that I felt an inner urge to begin a life review, to search back through every experience, every decision, and every turn I had taken to see how I'd ended up where I was now at. Somehow, I knew that it had to be me who had brought me to this place. It wasn't God I blamed, because I knew without doubt that God is Love. But I had been blaming others, as it seemed to be their words, their actions, and their behavior toward me that were causing me pain. Yet, deep inside, I somehow knew this couldn't be true either.

In my office, I had shelves overhead, and they were filled with cards from friends throughout the years, expressing to me their love and their respect, sharing their hearts, letting me know that I had been a gift in their lives, and thanking me for being who I am. Time and again, I asked myself *who* were they seeing? If this were truly me, why couldn't I see this in myself?! Somehow, somewhere I had been blinded to seeing the truth about myself, and I had to find out why!

Throughout the first year of searching, I had written and seen many things, but what I saw brought more pain and a deep sense of regret and powerlessness to change the effects of the experiences in my life. In starting over again, laying it all out, transferring it from the deep recesses of inner pain to paper, exposing it all to really look at it, as I entered the second year of writing, I began to see things differently. As I did, I began to feel a release from the guilt I had carried so long in trying so hard to simply hang onto this self I thought I was.

That is what I had been doing all along—rebelliously fighting and struggling against being jammed into this tight, little box into which I did not fit, so busy fighting that I was not looking where I was going. The struggle, the resistance, and the rebelling against everything and everyone around me had weakened me to the point I just didn't want to be here any longer. It now felt it was all for nothing and had gained me nothing but a deeper box to climb out of, one that I had made myself. There were no thoughts of suicide, just a sense of resignation to just wait it out until the end came at last to set me free. In the days to come, I would find that the end was coming, but it was not physical death but, rather, a death to the lies I had believed and lived by my whole life. Here was where the source within me, the One I call Spirit, led me to Truth.

Spirit's voice within began to interject peace in the middle of my long litany of painful thoughts, providing answers and insights like nothing I have ever heard before. So many times, I remember sitting back in my chair and saying out loud, "*Wow.*" And I wanted more. One or two hours in the morning stretched into three, four, or more hours every day. I loved being alone in my cave just listening, as I was beginning to see and understand.

When I shared this new experience with a friend, attempting to explain what I had found, she asked me, "How do you know this Voice isn't just your own thoughts?"

The only answer that I had was that the things I heard were like nothing I had ever heard or thought of in my life. Soft and peaceful, but always strong and powerful, providing answers that I had never been able to find before, this Voice began to follow me everywhere. I would get sudden insights while driving, often having to pull over so I could write them down, as I did not want to forget any of this amazing truth and wisdom I was being shown.

While I was submerged in all of these new, exciting discoveries, the onslaught on the outside began to intensify. My husband began to repeatedly ask, "What are you *doing* in there?! Why aren't you out here with me?!"

Though I didn't recognize it then, I now know these questions were full of fear; I was withdrawing, but he didn't know where I was going, only that it was away from him. My attempts to share the wonder I was finding was cut off after a few words, and I soon realized that he was afraid to hear. But I didn't stop. He no longer frightened me—I knew I had found something that I would never give up, not for him or anyone else. I had found peace, for the first time in my life. And having found peace, I wasn't about to give it up.

One day while reading, I find a quote in the book of Thomas: "Whoever has not known himself has known nothing, but whoever has known himself has simultaneously achieved knowledge about the depths of all things."

Still not having a clue who I was, I wanted this, and I wanted it now! So, who am I?! It was here that I increased my search. This was a time when I stopped to really look at each phase of my life, not just write it down and go on. And I mean I stopped and looked. This time, I wasn't seeing through a victim's eyes but, rather, with clear vision. And soon I found myself comforting the little girl I found, who was so lonely and confused, and understanding the teenage girl who had so valiantly fought for her freedom and letting her know I understood.

I recognized the mistake I had made in turning my life over to others' hands to shape and mold and that doing so had brought me nothing but dissatisfaction and misery. In always trying to please others, I had sacrificed my own heart's desires and happiness to give others theirs. As I lingered, looked, and started to truly see, I began to let the past go, holding onto the lessons learned. It was in releasing what I saw was no longer true—recognizing that, unseen and ignored, the past would continue to scream out for my attention, interjecting itself into my every present moment, and influencing my future—that a heavy burden was being lifted.

As layer after layer was removed, an image began to appear, and I didn't recognize her. She was like no one I had ever met and definitely not the face I saw in the mirror every day. She was happy; she was free; she loved to laugh and have fun; and, most importantly, she loved everyone simply for who they were, most of all me. She was so beautiful, and I fell completely in love with her. It wasn't long before I began to understand that she was me, the true me, the me that had always been me, longing to be free to simply *be*. It was her all along that my friends had been seeing. Wanting nothing more than to spend more time with her, getting to know her better, I found that she kept disappearing from my sight; I would only catch glimpses of her now and then before she was gone. Feeling desperate, as I wanted her with me always, I asked myself why I kept losing sight of her beauty—my beauty—and I knew there were more thoughts of the past that kept butting in, obscuring my vision.

So I returned to my search, and I realized I now had to look at my relationship with my husband. Why had our road been so bumpy? Why we were at this dead-end road of pain and misery felt by both of us? Suddenly I knew! We had both brought the garbage from the past with us and dumped the whole stinking mess into our life together. We had brought our fears, our experiences and beliefs, and our failures and mistakes and unloaded. In my fear of rejection, I sought the familiar, a controller. In his fear, he sought to control everything and everyone around him and sought someone easy to control. A match made in heaven? More like in hell!

It had worked until one of us began to change. In my search to find myself, I was beginning to accept and love myself as the bits and pieces of past fear and guilt began to drop away. In this newfound sense of self, I was beginning to chafe against the control that was holding me back, and I no longer wanted to play this game. As the fear within me, which had made this relationship compatible, began to disappear, the controller was thrown into fear. He was fighting to regain control by bullying and verbal abuse, attempting to pull me back under his control. It had always worked before, so he was expecting it to work now. Now, it couldn't, because I was no longer who I had been in the past.

For me, this new insight had a downside as well. In seeing the part I had played in bringing the past into the present, leading to the destruction of our present and future, I again began experiencing great guilt. Guilt had been my ruling mentor all my life, so the acceptance of this heavy guilt was natural. For some time, it caused me to overlook how far I had come, as I listened as guilt told me the failure of this marriage was on me. Weeks later, still struggling with this guilt, I heard the words, "*Guilt is fear's loudest voice.*" And, to ever be free, I must learn guilt's voice well, so that when I heard it, I would recognize it and could then simply walk away. While I believed this to be true, I found it easier said than done.

To ease guilt's voice, I began spending more time with my husband in an attempt to make amends for the harm I had caused. As I endured his bullying, I began to find that his words meant nothing to me anymore. They simply had no effect, as, along with this new love I had found for myself, a new self-respect and a newfound sense of self-worth was forming. Instead of taking offense, I began to look at him with full understanding of what he was doing in his fear and felt compassion instead of pain. Instead of calming him, this acceptance made him angry, and he would increase his verbal abuse in an attempt to break me, to get me to respond in anger or cry in pain—anything so that he felt he was again in control. Those days were gone.

As the days went on, I began to merge more fully into my true self, the self I had seen and fallen in love with, this self that my false perception had kept prisoner so long. Now, I had to find out how I could allow her to come out and finally be who I am. This time, when I found her, I would spend more time with her, learning who she was and allowing myself to trust her, because, like I had with others, I knew I had been holding her at arm's length, afraid to get too close. She was new to me, and although I loved her already, I resisted surrendering in trust to the unknown. The answer was to simply visit her more often, begin to invite her out to play and just enjoy the time I spent with her. This I did, and this I will continue to do.

Throughout all of this, I was finding that the key to living, truly living and loving life, is to know the true self. This isn't easy, as the self we are and came to be has been slowly buried under who we are told we are, who we are told to be and must be to survive in this new realm we find ourselves in. So, along the way, we lose our true identity to become like everyone else, holding the same fears, beliefs, and thoughts that we have been taught. This hurts not only us, but also everyone around us, everywhere we go, leaving a wake of destruction in our path, along with bits and pieces of ourselves.

In journeying back, I may have experienced the pain of guilt and regret, but I had to go there to find the bits and pieces of myself that I had left behind, if I ever hoped to be whole. Now recognizing the value of my search, despite the pain, or maybe motivated by it, I have to go on to find my true self and keep her with me always. And so I did.

Chapter 16

EENY, MEENY, MINY, MOE ... I'LL KEEP YOU AND LET THE OTHERS GO!

You can't really have lasting confidence until you locate and remove the beliefs that make you doubt yourself.

—Marissa Peer

It wasn't long before I could see that releasing myself from the acquired beliefs of others is freedom and a step toward peace, both of which I had been searching for all my life. To find this freedom and peace, I was told that I had to first release myself from my own buried beliefs about myself before I could fully move into the freedom to be. In other words, I had to accept myself as myself so that others could as well. It was past time to stop comparing myself to others and time to just accept myself as my true self and be who I am. The world doesn't need copycats now—those, like me, who have followed in the footsteps of those around me. The world needs each of us to be our own unique, individual self to reach those who are lost in pain and in a way that they can relate to, helping them find their own unique, individual self and the way to peace. It became so clear to me that I can't do this by being a carbon copy of others, because this dims my individual light and causes me to just blend in, never to be seen or used to help others. Shine on, I was told, shine on and be a light to those around you by being who you truly are. It was time to get to work, finding what imprisoning beliefs I was clinging to and transforming them into truth.

A new search began, the search for the false beliefs about myself that were holding me captive. There is no belief that is neutral; and I now knew that, as I believe, so shall I be. So what exactly was I believing? It wasn't long before beliefs began to appear, as one by one, they were exposed for me to see. It wasn't a pretty sight, but a belief seen is a belief that can be changed or removed.

The first hidden belief that appeared was, "It's all your fault." That one was not hard to find, as I had already reviewed my first few years on earth. And it appeared to be just that—*all my fault!* First up, the demise of my parents' marriage and the end of all the happiness and fun my family had experienced before my existence. If I hadn't been born, life would have been good. This belief had lodged itself successfully in the deep recesses of my mind, and I had carried it with me through every experience thereafter. Looking back, no matter what happened, with whom, or the circumstances, if the result appeared to be negative, I believed that it was somehow all my fault. If only I hadn't said, if only I hadn't done, if only I had been different, prettier, smarter, more giving, less selfish, the list was endless, always going back to the finger pointed at me—my own finger. The guilt was crippling; even when others did not blame me, I blamed myself.

As I relived episode after episode where I criticized, judged, and condemned myself for simply being myself, I could see that this belief had to go for me to ever allow myself to be who I am without fear of ruining anything and everything that came into my life. Up until now, from my viewpoint, I had ruined every relationship I had ever had, including the one I was in. Wanting nothing more than to be free, I asked for help in releasing this belief.

As soon as I did, instructions began flowing in. First, I was told that I was to praise myself every day—to speak the same words to myself that I spoke every morning to Spirit, telling myself that I was loved, thanking myself for the progress I had made, and being thankful for the goodness and abundance in my life. Then, I was to stop avoiding looking in mirrors, something I had done all my life, and to fully look and tell myself how beautiful I was, inside and out, and then, throughout the day, to praise myself for my understanding and my inherent goodness, if only to myself. In other words, I was to be thankful for *me* and praise *me* for truly being in my life! Every day, I was to be conscious of every negative thought about myself and to replace each one with a positive.

It wasn't long before my perception began to change, both about myself and in every situation I was in. Everything became brighter, lighter, clearer, as I quit blaming myself and began to see people and circumstances as they truly are. As I did, I could see that negative outcomes weren't really all that negative. And if they appeared to be, they were not "all my fault." Finally beginning to feel the freedom to walk in the beauty of who I truly am, I continued the search.

The next belief, which went hand in hand with the first, was that, "I'm a failure." My life seemed to be nothing but a series of mistakes resulting in failures. Failure as a child, failure as a teenager, failure in obtaining any dream I've ever held, failure in marriage, failure in my church. And as I looked back, I was seeing nothing but failure after failure. This is how I had been viewing my life—as one big failure. But as I moved toward discovering who I truly am, I began to see that there are no failures, only experiences within which I was learning and able to go out and try again. This is how we learn—if we choose to learn at all. There was nothing to be forgiven for, as no one has been holding anything against me but me. Looking at past "failures" in a totally new and different perspective, I could now be thankful for my perceived past mistakes, as I would not be who I am today without them or know what I now know. There are few people who I've met to whom I cannot say, "Been there, done that," and be able to relate with them as they share their life, holding no judgment but loving understanding. This is a valuable healing tool and one I would not have if I had not experienced all that I had. So, I am thankful. Most of all I'm thankful that I could finally see the truth, as in seeing, I began to see all things differently, including, and most importantly, my own self.

The revelation of false, negative beliefs was far from over. I would continue to be amazed at how my false beliefs had built upon each other, as the next belief I saw was that, "I'm a nobody." This belief was based on my own view of societal dictates on education and my belief that I could never be "somebody," because I did not have a college degree. Not having this piece of paper meant, in my belief, that I was less than, with little or nothing of value to offer. And I didn't just see this about myself; I also believed that everyone else saw me the same way. Instead of seeing and appreciating me, they only saw was what I was lacking. When I was shown this, I was also shown a picture of myself that I would begin to see over and over again—that my education was in life, the PhD I held was in the richness of the experiences that I have had that few others have ever before experienced. Through these experiences, I was now in a position where there were few who I met that I could not relate to, understand, and help to heal from their own mistaken beliefs. In seeing the richness of my education, I now saw that it was plentiful and valuable, far more costly than money could buy. And I knew I wouldn't trade it for anything the world had to offer.

As I talked with my husband one night, he commented on the wisdom in the words I spoke but told me that, while what I said was amazing and valuable, "Nobody is going to listen to you with no letters behind your name." Although he'd meant to criticize, I had to laugh. I now knew what I had to offer and told him so. In explaining, I suddenly saw letters appear after my name, and those letters were L.I.F.E. Laughing even harder, I knew that this belief was well on its way out. And with my degree posted on the wall of my heart, it was time to go out and be all that I am here to be. There was a position that had been created for me that few were qualified to fill.

Beginning to see myself in a new light, my confidence began to grow. As it did, I began to share the rich knowledge of life that I now knew I had obtained and could feel myself finally beginning to breathe. By this time, I was beginning to understand that how I was feeling was created by the thoughts I was thinking. Others were not looking at me as "less than." Only I was, causing me to hold my breath in fear of judgment. With this new change in belief and my confidence rising, I increasingly enjoyed being my true self. With shoulders back and head held high, I was beginning to feel strong.

There was one more belief that had to be seen—one that, again, tied in with the rest. This was the belief that, "I have nothing of any value to say." Who was I to speak up, share the innate richness of wisdom and insight that I had within? It had been ignored, criticized and rejected before, so was I willing to take the chance now, only to experience the pain of rejection again? Throughout my life I had answered no; I was not willing. And look where it had gotten me—at a dead end with nothing to look forward to, because I never spoke up.

This belief that I had nothing of value to say had to go! Was this easy? Oh my no! One does not simply eliminate a long-held fearful belief. It took time, practice, and an awareness of this fear whenever I chose to speak.

Knowing I had to bravely walk through this fear to rid myself of it, I began asking myself, "What is the worst that can happen if I share what has been given me to say?" I quickly found that the repercussions did not appear as deadly as I had once imagined, and I began to speak. Maybe just a few words, but each word built up my confidence until I could speak more often, more confidently, as I saw that I was heard and listened to.

In time, no matter what the reaction of others to the words I spoke, I found that it no longer mattered. I was finally speaking, and it felt so good to finally be free to use my voice. Yes, I was on the road to freedom.

Clearly, I was being shown that a belief is a very stubborn thing, firmly embedded as habits of thought in the mind, as a belief is nothing more than the same thought we think over and over again. As we do so, these beliefs establish a deep groove within the mind that will stubbornly run along its track, expecting no interruptions and despising those that do appear and attempt to derail them. Established beliefs do not like their familiar routine changed, rerouted, ignored, or disrupted and will erupt in anger, resentment, and turmoil as they struggle to get back onto their familiar, well-worn groove to control once again. Things must be this way or that way, or it is wrong. People must do this or that, or they are wrong. My day must go according to the habitual belief that I have formed, or it is wrong, and it cannot and will not be accepted. When a belief is allowed to gain control, its deep groove gets deeper and deeper, eventually resulting in a chasm so deep that it is buried from the consciousness like an unseen wound that produces an unrecognized pain. Left unattended and unacknowledged long enough, the wound is allowed to fester and rot, eventually affecting the whole thought system and resulting in the death of our quality of life.

Walking through this dark valley, where false beliefs lingered like ghosts, ghosts from the past that were haunting my life now, I moved onto higher ground. There, I began to see and understand that each false belief was like a hovering tiny particle of fear that believes it is here to keep me safe and protected from a cold, harsh, unloving world. To them, the smaller I could keep myself, the more hidden beneath their protection, the safer and more secure I would be. Looking at each belief with new insight, I knew that I could not just reject or ignore them, pretending they did not exist, because this just made them more determined to be heard, their voices becoming louder as I tried to bury them deep in my psyche, the very place where they could do their worst harm. They had to go, as I did not need or want the protection that they offered and no longer wanted to be held back from becoming who I truly am. No, I had to look at them, accept that they were there, and recognize that their purpose was to hold me tightly gripped in fear. It was in seeing them that I could release their tentacles—let them go, telling them their job was done, and they were no longer needed. This is part of the lesson that I had to learn to ever be free.

As I was releasing the false, it seemed that the void was filling with the true. And with each release came peace and a literal sense of happiness, a lightness never felt before. With this as my guide, I began noticing how I felt throughout the day and found that my feelings were a safe guide. When I felt uneasy, angry, resentful, or sad, it was time to stop and examine what I had been thinking and which belief I had been seeing life through. When I felt happy and lighthearted, I would also take notice, and I began to understand that happiness meant I was thinking truth, whereas discomfort or pain meant I had somehow wandered off and had slipped back into the old groove of a false belief. Having had enough pain to last several lifetimes, it was past time to let go of the old and welcome the new and true, moving freer into whatever comes next.

Would I be able to continue dwelling in this peace and happiness I now found myself in? I guess the test would come in what was yet ahead. But now I was ready, having found the truth that was setting me free to be.

Chapter 17

TO TELL THE TRUTH, THE WHOLE TRUTH AND NOTHING BUT THE TRUTH, SO *HELP* ME GOD!

When you tell the truth, your story changes, and
when you change your story, your life is transformed.

—Mark Matousek

*W*ithin this newfound truth about myself, a desire began to grow within to find something I could feel passionate about and devote my life to. There were many things I felt strongly passionate about, and as I thought about all of them, I began to grow confused. Not knowing which one to choose, I heard I was to focus on one to shoot for, or I'd end up being like a shotgun shell spraying BBs all over that would wound but never hit the target. While understanding this analogy, I was still left in confusion.

I heard the Voice within get a little louder, this time startling me in its clarity. In the silence of my office, I heard that I had been a rebel without a cause for long enough, and I was about to be given one. My heart literally felt like it stopped at these words, not in fear but in anticipation, and I could no longer think or write, as I sat there wondering what this cause could be. My life flashed before me and I saw myself rebelliously fighting my way through life with no cause but to save myself, resulting in compounding the pain. Finally, with hesitation, I asked what this cause was.

Having waited until asked, the words came quickly. I was told that I was to speak the truth and, in speaking truth, set the captive free. These words so resonated with my heart that I began to cry. I had longed for this freedom, and now I was asked to give the very thing I most desired. In that moment, I knew this was it, what I had been searching for all my life, and I wanted to know more.

But following closely behind this life-changing experience came my own thoughts, asking me if I could possibly be serious. Who was I to tell the truth, the one who had buried my voice long ago? As my heart began to sink in discouragement, I was reassured that I was to simply trust; have faith, and I would find the courage to do what I had been asked to do.

Shortly after this, I was picking up food from a diner close to my workplace. As I got out of my car, I glanced over at a poster on the side of a bar next to my parking place. It was a picture of a long-haired blond woman, who looked a lot like me, sitting astride a Harley. The caption read, "The Original Rebel." Smiling, I thought, *Yup, that's me!* After picking up my food and driving away, I heard these words: *Rebel—really enjoying being everything life.* This new perception of rebel, a label assigned to me long ago and meant as a curse, was so liberating that I laughed all the way to work! Gone was the guilt and pain this label had caused for so long. I now saw a new and different sight of me in that moment. Truth is spoken to us through a myriad of different mediums. And for me, it was the words on a bar poster that helped set me free!

Shortly after this, I read a quote by William Shakespeare: "No legacy is so rich as honesty." It was like a confirmation. Right then I knew that I wanted to be known and remembered as someone others could always trust to tell the truth. At the same time, still remembering it takes courage to be so honest, I began to look around me to find those who had the courage I believed I lacked. Although I watched and listened to everyone I knew, I found no one who had this courage to be honest and truthful, and I asked why. The answer was clear. I saw that everyone wants to belong; to be viewed as nice, kind, and agreeable; and to be liked; yet everyone, including me, was lying.

It was in really listening to others that I learned that most of us play a game of subtle hints, half-truths, and flat-out lies, afraid the truth will bring with it criticism, rejection, or judgment, and I was guilty as well. So many times I had put sugar coating on a crap load of lies, hoping to avoid an argument, a confrontation, all the terrible results I imagined would come from being truthful. In the meantime, no one really knew me. Nor did I even know myself. I'd been getting nothing and going nowhere, as how could I trust someone who was not honest?

It was truth that answered when I realized I didn't trust—not myself and not others. Once again looking back at my own life, I heard myself saying things to others just to make them feel good. Most was not truth. But having lived in fear for so long and just wanting to be accepted, my habit was to lie. So I believed that others were lying to me as well. Lying might be considered kind, but it is not truth, and lies never help anyone. Either I was going to tell the truth, or I'd tell a lie. There were no gray areas, and I had to decide if I was going to be honest or if I was going to be a liar. Seeing this game I had been playing shook me to my core, and I made the decision to stop playing games and be honest, both with myself and with others. Did I have the courage? Truthfully, I wasn't sure. Yet I knew that I wanted to fulfill this cause to speak the truth, so I yelled, "HELP me, God!"

To tell the truth, I knew that I must first know the truth. And I now knew that the truth was not my beliefs, my opinions, my theology, my ideas, or my thoughts but, rather, something found deep within my very core being. Learning that I could tell if something I heard or thought was the truth by how the words resonated within me, I went searching, asking for help in finding the truth I was seeking. With this as my focus, I found it was all around me—in random quotes, a chance article, television shows, and always in listening within and in listening to others. Literally surrounded, I was amazed that I had never seen it all before.

It was in purposefully listening to others that I was usually able to hear the truth in them, truth they were hiding behind the words they spoke. In doing so, an old gift rose up inside of me, a gift I had buried long ago as a child due to reprimands and punishment, and it was the gift of knowing. As I listened intently below the words, I knew what others were hiding from, truth unrecognized even by them.

Asking for help in how to share what I was seeing, I began to ask questions, questions others had to think about before answering. And many began to see the truth for themselves. Other times, I would tell a story about someone I knew who had gone through a similar experience and how it could best be rectified in a constructive way.

One new friend, who didn't know me well, always avoided looking at me, focusing her attention on others we were with but never me, and I couldn't figure out why. One evening, she finally looked directly at me and truthfully said, "You make me uncomfortable, because it's like you can see right inside of me."

Laughing, I said, "I can."

After that, our friendship grew; she understood she had nothing to hide, as I had nothing to judge. There is no judgment in truth, just gentle understanding and acceptance. Truth is never here to judge but to help us be who we truly are and, in being, be free.

This was becoming fun. I was soon experimenting everywhere I went—at home, at work, with a stranger at a store, with a neighbor next door, and with friends. Just to listen and be honest in return.

In my exuberance, I began practicing being honest at home with my husband, and it was here that I continued to learn. This practice was both difficult and easy—difficult, as I was not accustomed to telling him the truth, having always hidden my thoughts and feelings for fear of attack, but easy because I no longer cared what he thought or said about me. In the beginning, I pussyfooted around, still a bit on edge, as this truth speaking was still new to me after so many years of hiding behind lies. But as time went on, I learned that, if I listened closely to the words he spoke, he would relax, and we could honestly share. During these times, it was easy, and I found him listening and could sense him soften, but there were other times he would hear something that I said and react in anger. Soon, I learned that these were the times that I had hit a nerve and shared something he didn't want to see. Discomfort was not my goal, but truth can be revealing, and I was learning that I had just spoken the truth by his reaction.

He began to say, "Who *are* you?!" more and more often. And I couldn't answer, because I still wasn't sure myself. Unknown to me, the outer shell, the personality I had formed based on the past, was dissolving, melting around me. As it did, I was emerging, unrecognizable even to myself. The light within was slowly melting the waxen shell I had formed around me, removing the barrier that had long hidden my truth. While I didn't see it, as I grew accustomed to living in this light of truth, it was blinding to him.

There is a reason people are sworn to tell the truth in a court hearing. The words are now spoken robotically, with no meaning attached, but the words remain powerful when spoken. "I swear to tell the truth, the whole truth, and nothing but the truth, so *help* me God!" In other words, give me the courage and the strength to stand before the world and speak the truth, regardless of the ramifications.

What is the truth? The opposite of a lie, which is fear camouflaged. To me, truth is love, and all else emanates from this one truth. Be it my thoughts, my words, or my actions, only the truth holds any power, any healing, any life, as all life is created to be an extension of love. If truth is love and a lie fear, which do I choose to base my life upon? Love or fear? A lie only succeeds in birthing more lies to cover the first lie, and fear is multiplied instead of love. We know when we lie. It never feels good, even when the intentions are good, because we know it is not the truth. And we are created to always tell the truth, and nothing but the truth, because we *are* truth; we *are* love.

At times, truth can hurt, but I was finding that it is a hurt that heals, like the pain experienced after surgery when a foreign mass has been removed from the body, making it whole and complete once again. Truth is the Sword that heals by cutting away what does not belong, leaving only truth to live and prosper in our life.

In finding truth during this review of my life story, I found I was at peace and not only at peace, but renewed, rejuvenated, and excited, finding a new purpose in moving forward. This purpose was to seek, to think, to speak, and to live the truth and nothing but the truth, with the ever-present help within.

By now, I knew that there are many ways of sharing the truth, and words are only one form. Every action speaks and speaks clearly, heard by all who see. "Actions speak louder than words" is a common saying and truer than most understand. It was not enough to simply tell the truth. I must also live the truth. And if I do not live the truth, then the words I speak are empty and void of any true meaning. When I speak, I must back up what I say by how I live, as words become unnecessary when truth is lived. If words need to be used, then I will be asked to speak. If not, I must simply allow my life to reveal the truth, as "seeing is believing." So this is what I have determined to do.

As my search for truth continued (and it always will), there was a growing sense of excitement. I found that truth leads to joy, and joy was leading me to love—the love of everything and everyone. It was like a door had opened and, as I was brave enough to finally walk through, the cloud of lies that I had been hiding behind for so long began to clear. Here, I could see that lies hide us and do not serve anyone. And I wanted to clearly and truthfully see myself as I am and all others as they are, which is lovely, pure, and divine.

Telling the truth was one of the hardest things I had ever done, and one of the best things I would ever do to help set myself free from who I thought I was into who I truly am. All it took was willingness on my part and asking for help to set this captive free. It was a new step in waking up, a new way to see the experience I am having in a clearer, brighter way.

Chapter 18

THE METAMORPHOSIS: WHAT HAPPENED TO THE WORM?!

When we are no longer able to change a situation,
we are challenged to change ourselves.

—Viktor Frankl

*A*s I began to discover more and more about who I truly am—and understand how my beliefs and thoughts were limiting and holding me captive—I continued to change. Slowly and subtly, a transformation was taking place within. And while I did not see it, others did, particularly those closest to me. My husband was especially aware of this change, as he was still choosing to look at me as the worm, his attitude being "once a worm, always a worm." When the butterfly began to slowly emerge, he no longer recognized me and began to tell me so. The transformation frightened him.

And I understood, as I barely recognized myself any longer. But unlike him, I was seeing the beauty in who was emerging. The fear I had clung to for so long was very slowly being replaced with confidence, and with confidence came courage. Within this inner confidence emerged new sight as well. Looking at my husband with new eyes, I could see how he, too, was suffering and could experience this happy confidence for himself. After all, who wants to live a life of misery and suffering when one does not have to?! In my newfound courage, I began to speak up, both for myself and to share what I was finding.

The response? Another, "Who *are* you?!" and, "Quit preaching. I don't want to hear it." Excited about what was happening, I just wanted to share, not preach. But my voice was not appreciated. Same ole story as in the past, just a different setting.

In fairness, I had entered the relationship as the worm he had come to know. Like a worm, I had kept myself hidden, wrapped securely in my cocoon where I felt safe, and he had never known me. This was what he had seen. And my actions and lack of action backed this image up. By hiding my voice, I backed off into my cocoon every time I was confronted with a challenge. And in our relationship, there were many. Keeping silent, I only reinforced within myself the image of the worm, as I had had no self-respect and no sense of worth. Silently I endured and resented both of us. The downhill spiral had started soon after we were married, and I had contributed to the descent by my silence.

During my hibernation period, I had begun listening to my A Course in Miracles tapes every morning while getting ready for the day. In anger, and what I was to later recognize as fear, my husband would storm out of the house to his barn as soon as he heard the tape. In truth, listening was drawing me closer to him, as I was learning so much about love. But he was too afraid to get close enough to find out.

As time continued, and the transformation continued within me, his fear and anger began fermenting. One day, in front of others, he yelled, "What are others going to think if they walk in the house and hear a man's voice in the bathroom with you?!" Sure that he was joking, as it was just a voice on a cassette tape, I began to laugh. When he yelled, "This isn't funny," and stormed away,

I realized he was serious and suddenly knew that he was jealous; he was losing me to an unknown, unseen entity that he had no idea how to compete with. This fear only fueled his onslaught of criticism and disparaging remarks, but I found that I no longer cared.

Recognizing this, he upped the ante even more. The verbal attacks became ridiculous, and he would choose company to fortify his courage in voicing his fear. Others would shake their heads, seeing what he couldn't see.

As I had never been one to fight in front of others, knowing it made them uncomfortable, one day I'd had enough. By now I was feeling safe within an inner world of peace and began confronting his every word with simple truth in a quiet, logical manner. When he found out there was not one accusation that I did not have a valid, simple answer for, he went on a rampage of false accusations and taunts, succeeding in making himself look immature and ridiculous in front of others. What he had hoped would hurt me was only hurting him. While all of this sounds uncomfortable, I was seeing what good practice it was, as I was learning how to live within my inner peace and, within this peace, learning that nothing could affect me. I was actually growing stronger for the practice and began to enjoy the challenge. I'm sure there was an easier way, but, hey, when had I ever chosen the easy way? Seeing this, I laughed out loud, as I saw the rebel in action and loved her for her strength. But she sure had a ways to go in wisdom.

Entertaining as it was, there were times it could also be draining. I asked myself why I was spending any time at all with him. In my solitude, I had a Friend—one who loved to listen to me and shared richness in return. My husband clearly did not enjoy my company, and, although he was always complaining that I wasn't spending enough time with him, he was letting me know with every word and action that my very presence irritated him. Finally, I realized that he still thought he could bully me into relinquishing this peace I had found to become what he wanted. But it was too late. The worm was transforming, and she could no longer be forced back into her cocoon, as it was rapidly disintegrating. The butterfly was making her way out to fly free, and I was beginning to really like this new me. If he didn't, then I could enjoy my own company. Making the decision that I had had enough, I began to simply stay away, choosing to no longer expend so much energy to counter his verbal blows and to use this energy to strengthen myself instead.

This did not entirely end the discomfort, as I was often on edge, especially in the mornings. My office, where I communed and wrote, was upstairs, facing the barn he now practically lived in, and he would stand in the doorway staring down at my window, hands on hips, legs spread apart. I could literally feel the animosity and angry energy directed my way. Here, I asked myself why I remained in this environment. In answer, I knew that I was still hoping that the transformation taking place in me could transform our relationship as well. I was determined to keep my hope alive.

Somewhere, in the middle of all of this, I had a sudden release from the past. For years, I had awakened in the middle of the night to thoughts of past sexual escapades for which I felt thoroughly ashamed. These memories haunted me. One day, in a sudden instant, the truth came to me—the past was gone, over, a search for meaning and nothing more. I was set totally free!

Feeling exhilarated and excited, I wanted to share and saw that my husband was alone in his barn, so I went out to join him. Why, with all that had been said and done the past several years I thought he would listen, I was too excited to even think about it. Taking it slow, we made small talk. And then the door opened, as we began talking about the past. Beginning to tell him about the wonderful freedom I had found, explaining about the horrible burden I had been carrying for so many years, I shared how I was now free and how wonderful it felt and how happy I was.

His reaction was sudden and totally unexpected. He exploded. "Who *are* you?" he demanded, shouting at me that he had always thought I was so innocent. Why hadn't I shared my past? Why had I lied and deceived him? He called me names meant to hurt.

While surprised at his response, this barrage did not even faze me. I was so lost in this ecstasy of freedom that it felt like I was enveloped in a cloud of perfect peace. Feeling no need to defend myself, as I now knew there was nothing to defend, I felt like I was listening to his spiteful words from a distance. They just didn't matter.

Later, alone with myself, I realized that he thought I was rubbing sex in his face, as our own sex life had deteriorated along with our relationship. It hadn't been my intent at all. I was merely sharing my experience. But he couldn't see. In that moment, I felt great sadness for both of us, truly seeing the deep chasm for what it was.

Again, my thoughts turned to leaving. I wanted to find a sanctuary away from the drama and turmoil—somewhere I could totally submerge myself into this place where my heart was calling me. The call was becoming louder and louder every day, and my total withdrawal scared him. The more I withdrew, the more he asked me to join him in his barn.

Recognizing this was his safe space, a place where he felt secure, I finally decided to go, as I still believed there was some way to mend this relationship. Praying for a miracle, I was to find that he only invited me into his den to blame and accuse, to find fault with how I was ruining his life. Later I had a good laugh and shook my head, as I caught another glimpse of the rebel, determined to win, refusing to give up, yelling the whole time, "You can't make me quit!" She had more to learn, for sure.

Finally, I was tired of living this dual life of peace and war, and I found my voice. A month before our twentieth anniversary, I told him that, if he didn't change how he was treating me, I was leaving. His face registered total shock and fear and he said, "Don't do this to me, please."

Totally caught off guard, I stared at him amazed, suddenly understanding that he had no idea what he was doing to us.

Shaking my head in disbelief, I asked him what we had between us, as long gone was any respect, love, tenderness, or concern for the relationship, yet he wanted to hold onto it?! He gave me no answer, and I again explained that I would not continue to live with the continual barrage of criticism and that, while I longed to mend our relationship, I couldn't do it by myself, as it takes two. It wasn't an ultimatum. All I asked was that he honor and respect me, honor and respect us, and be willing to take another look at how we had gotten to this stranglehold of pain.

His shock and fear were too great, and he wasn't listening. Instead, he took this as a line drawn in the sand and began preparing for war in his thoughts. Unaware, I walked away with the hope that he would think about this, and we could begin to mend the bridge between us, finding a way back to each other once again.

Reviewing this chapter of my life, it was in a moment of revelation that I understood the look of shock on my husband's face when I told him that I wanted to be treated better or I was leaving. To me, all that I was asking was for was what I had been deprived of as a child—honor, respect, and acceptance. But all he heard were the words, "I'm leaving." With these words rushed back all of his childhood memories of being left and abandoned; he had been abandoned as a child both by his mother and then his father, leaving him wondering what was wrong with him that no one could love him. His pain and fear had been intense, and I had seen it on his face.

Suddenly, I remembered words from ACIM—every word and action is either love or a call for love. And in a moment of clarity, I knew that his angry outbursts had been a call for the love he had felt deprived of all his life. Like a little child seeking the attention and reassurance so desperately needed, by throwing temper tantrums with verbal outbursts, my husband had been calling out for love—to be told he was okay and that he wasn't a failure, but rather, worthy to be seen, recognized, and accepted and, most of all, loved.

From this moment on, I would only see him as who he truly is—a man who is gentle, kind, wise, and strong. All were attributes I had seen from time to time, but they had been hidden so long in his own cocoon of fear that he no longer knew who he was. The role he was playing was patterned on a lifetime of chosen beliefs and habits that he had used to protect himself, habits that had destroyed every relationship he had ever had. My heart went out to him. As it did, I felt the burden of resentment and pain released from my mind, leaving me in peace. It wasn't that I had to live with this man, but in truly seeing him, I could accept and love him, even if from a distance.

Our problems were the result of our thoughts—who we believe we are based on the past that we carried through life with us like a precious cargo. But these thoughts, brought into the here and now, were the barrier to true understanding that could build a strong foundation of union. We were continually pushing each other away in an effort to protect ourselves and all based on an image of who we thought we were. It was in this review that I saw all the self-inflicted pain, causing me to shake my head at the insanity of what we had been doing to each other and to ourselves. Oh yes, there is much to be learned by reviewing the past, taking with us the lessons learned before letting the past go—gone and left to rest in peace where it belongs.

For a while longer, I would continue to stay where I was, but change was on the horizon. In the meantime, I would continue to honor who I am, knowing that the true me was growing stronger, bolder, and ready to be who she truly was and had always been. Wings not yet unfurled but beginning to slowly break free from the bondage of the self-protective cocoon, the butterfly was emerging, and with or without me, she was ready to fly! Would I join her? I was about to find out!

Chapter 19

EVERYONE IS OUR TEACHER: I'M SURROUNDED!

Some will open your heart; others will open your eyes.

—C. C. Aurel

*A*s I continued to learn and grow, one day I read an article that mentioned "the paralysis of analysis." As I continued to read, I was about to be shown much about myself. Psychology had always fascinated me, and I had taken myself on an in-depth study of the subject, absorbing everything I could find. Yet, when I read this article, I could see that I was always analyzing in every situation and with every person I met, seeking what was wrong that needed to be fixed. Asking if this was paralyzing my ability to know the truth, I was told that it was. When talking with anyone, if I was so busy analyzing, which meant I was thinking instead of listening, I wasn't hearing the voice within every heart. While psychology has its strengths, its focus is on the human-conditioned mind, not the heart within, and it was the heart of a person that I wanted to meet, to know, and to hear. In that moment, I determined to put all analytical thoughts aside and focus only on observing and intently listening to everyone and everything around me.

Taking this purpose with me, I began to encounter teachers in everyone I met and in everything I encountered—teachers who had always been there, but I hadn't been listening. From the frogs in the spring, I learned the beauty and wonder of life, as they sang their song of joy and thanksgiving for warmth and simply being alive. From the robins in the spring, I learned the joy of the falling rain, as they sang their song of gratitude for the abundance the rain would bring. This was truly an amazing experience. I began to literally feel the beauty in every encounter I had.

Life is all about learning to remember what we have forgotten, and we are given ample opportunities to learn from what and who is around us, if we listen. Everyone and everything are teachers, and they come into our life to share truth, although most are unaware. It is within relationships where we find some of our richest learning experiences. From the people I met, I began to learn what to do to be successful, happy, and abundant and what not to do to avoid pain, misery, and fear. Very literally, I was surrounded by teachers with valuable lessons to share. In opening my mind up to listen and observe, I found that I was seeing things, hearing things, and knowing things about others, about myself, and about life that I could not have seen, heard, or known if my thoughts had been busy analyzing. By choosing to turn my thoughts off when talking with others and focusing only on what was being said, heart to heart, I was seeing truth like never before.

Teaching moments often came when I realized that I was literally looking into a mirror with everyone I met. One of my first lessons was in looking into the mirror of my relationship with my husband. I saw that he was mirroring to me my own lack of self-worth and self-respect by treating me as I saw myself. *Ouch!* That hurt! How could I expect from him what I was denying myself? This was a very valuable lesson from someone I had never viewed as a teacher until that moment. It helped me begin to remove the blame I had placed on him and do the inner work of healing my own self-perception.

It was then that I began really listening to him. As I did, I began to see the mask he wore to hide his fear behind. Always appearing confident, in control, and having an answer for everything, he came across as cocky, arrogant, and self-centered. This was driving others away, including me. His fear of being vulnerable and open to possible pain was too great, so he hid who he was where no one could see.

Again, I was looking in a mirror. Recognizing his mask and seeing what he was hiding, I had to ask myself what I was hiding behind the mask I wore. Finally daring to look, I saw great fear—fear that if others could see me, they would disapprove, criticize, condemn, and reject me. I saw that I had long ago donned a mask of confidence to hide my vulnerability from others. Seeing this, by the lesson taught to me by my husband, I understood that I could only remove this mask by finding and loving myself. As I did, bit by bit, I was able to begin to lift the mask I had long worn. And I found that, when I did, others began to relate to and understand me, as they now saw a real person, just like them, who lived with the same fears and questions that they did. This began to open the door to true relationships.

Through these lessons, how I saw others began to change. I found that I could sense when another was not being who he or she truly was; to find the person, I had to listen, both within and without. Knowing there was a real person behind that mask, having lived behind my own, I was determined to find out who others truly were. Listening was the key to finding the treasures that lie hidden within us all—listening and receiving what treasures I find. What an amazing journey I was about to take!

Teachers were literally everywhere, and I recognized that many were the women in my life. These were teachers I recognized, as they reminded me of myself. So many had never taken the time to cultivate self-love and self-appreciation and sought this love and appreciation from a man to fill the void. As I watched, I saw some who would exert so much pressure on a man to fulfill her intense need for love that the man finally exploded from the pressure, harming her physically and emotionally before leaving her completely. Others never removed their masks; the man fell in love with an imposter, and as the man saw who he had really married, he felt deceived and would leave. To exert so much pressure on another to provide for us what we can only give to our self is to drive others away. Lesson learned.

Still watching, I would learn how harmful expectations are—expectations that another would provide what we were not giving to ourselves. When expectations are not met, blame begins, and anger and resentment are born, accomplishing nothing and destroying much. Seeing myself reflected in so many helped set me free from a pattern of self-induced pain and misery. They taught me the rich lesson that to love oneself is the best thing we can do, for both our self and for others. It is in loving our own self that we quit demanding it from another and begin to give love instead. In the giving, we receive love in return. This was truly a lesson meant for me to see and learn, as I was living this lesson now.

The self-reflections continued, as more teachers appeared, some of them men. Whereas women are apt to become needy, men are more apt to become demanding. With no self-love within, they seek women who are easily controlled, are willing to be pushed around, and submit to any demand placed upon them in the man's search for his own fulfillment. Having no self-love, these men seek it from a woman who has no love to give, as she does not love herself. It never ends well, as the demanding man can never get enough, increasing the demands while the woman submits in fear. But all the while, the man knows that what he is receiving is fear and not the love he was seeking; and then he blames her. This was a lesson I had to learn, as, again, I was living with it myself. I could now understand that the man I was married to was seeking love, demanding love; and finding fear, he blamed me. Seeing that I could not provide for him what he did not have for himself relieved me of a very heavy load of guilt.

The lessons were endless. Next, I encountered teachers who totally lived in their imagined past victimization. In viewing themselves as a victim and blaming the past, they were clinging to it, basing their whole self-perception on a past that was long gone, except in their thoughts. Paying close attention, as I was seeing myself in them, I watched as self-perceived victims played out their story in different ways. Some repeated their story over and over again to anyone who would listen, as they had learned they would be seen and receive the attention they craved, but only as the victim they saw themselves as being. Shaking my head, I remembered how often I had shared my sorrowful story of the past, and I learned from them that I no longer wanted to be seen as a victim. And to be free, I had to let the past go and live free in the moment at hand.

The encounters were endless. I met some who lived in constant, continual emotional pain—their only goal being to heap their pain on others with the hope that it would ease their own pain. They were critical, condemning, and blaming and judged everything and everyone around them, seeing no good in anyone or anything, as they could see none within themselves. They gave what their thoughts were filled with, which was guilt, shame, pain, and blame, with the goal to give it away and lighten their own load. Seeing myself again, I had to acknowledge that I had long been critical and judging, giving guilt and blame to others, as this was what I had been taught and was holding inside. Learning much from these teachers, I was one step closer to the truth I had been searching for—the truth of who I truly am.

No matter where I went or who I was with, I was encountering teachers in everyone I met. From those in deep depression, I watched as they totally submerged themselves in past wrongs, recounting every imagined harm, blaming others, and missing out on the happiness available now, in this moment, and losing any hope for the future. They were literally putting themselves in a prison of self-pity and sure misery, driving others away by self-consumed thoughts. Taking this valuable lesson to heart, I began to get out of my own self-made prison of self-obsession and think of others, sending a card or an email to let someone know that I was thinking about him or her or making a phone call just to say hello. This lesson was rich.

As I watched and listened, I learned, and the lessons were plentiful and life transforming. They did this and felt pain, so I won't do that. They are doing this, and they are happy, so I will give what they are doing a try because I want to be happy. There were teachers who taught me to give the gift of a compliment and watch the receiver's face light up—even strangers in a store who shared a smile, giving me a gift of joy and teaching me to share a smile with others who I meet. The list of stories I would love to tell of teachers in my life is endless; some lessons were small but valuable, while others blew my thoughts to smithereens, never again to be found. All of these teachers have helped make my life so much more fulfilling, and I am grateful to them all. We are literally surrounded by those who have much to teach. And for all of those who have been sent to teach me, and for those to come, I give my heartfelt thanks.

When I began to look at others as my teachers, I found that I could observe without judgment, knowing that everyone is in my life to teach me something I need to know about myself. This made everyone valuable and worthwhile, having much to offer in the lessons they had to share. To see others in my life this way changed my perception from judgment to appreciation, from disdain to love for the gift they had given. It was all a matter of how I chose to look at things, turning the bad into good, the judgment into love and a new awareness that everyone is literally here for me and I for them. In every moment, with every word and action, we are all teaching others and should appreciate each other and the gifts we all have to share.

Now knowing that I, too, am a teacher, I began to wonder just what I had been teaching. This opened the door to a sudden understanding that I had been looking at my life all wrong. What if all the perceived mistakes I'd been making were all lessons I was here to teach? What if I had lived my life with purpose all along? As if in confirmation, I flashed back to the woman in the heroin den, watching as she was beaten and dragged across the room. What if she was there, in that moment, specifically for me to teach me that this was not the life I wanted for myself? After all, it was at that moment, while watching her, that I changed the course of my own life. What she shared with me appeared to be a mistake in her life, but she literally saved my life with what she was teaching me! Right then, I knew she was; there was no question that she was a teacher there just for me, and I was filled with gratitude for her gift! As my heart went out to her in thanksgiving, I hoped she could hear me, somewhere, somehow.

This blew my mind wide open, as old thoughts flew out of my mind and new thoughts flooded in about myself. This new vision of the magnitude of teaching moments we all give and receive in every moment transformed every harsh self-judgment I had held onto so tightly into the understanding of the gifts I had been giving. The seemingly good, the bad, the ugly, and the beautiful—all were gifts I had shared. Every word I spoke, every action I took, and every decision I made was teaching someone somewhere, and there was purpose in each and every one.

It was by looking at myself with eyes of love that I began to teach myself about myself from my own life. This beautiful picture before me was me. And how could I not love her, feel her heart, her yearning, her search for herself in every nook and cranny life presented to her to explore? My experiences had taught me to look at others with these eyes of love and see the innermost depths of them, to share my heart with their heart, and to see them as the precious being they truly are. Oh yes, we are all teachers, teaching ourselves and others as we learn.

In these teaching moments, seen within my own life, I experienced a new freedom. Now I knew that I could move ahead and look around me with new vision and would see things differently than I ever had before. Excited, I was ready to continue to seek what else there is to learn within reviewing my own life's chapters ahead, remembering that everyone is my teacher, including me.

Chapter 20

FACED WITH A DEAD END?
OR A NEW BEGINNING?

Change is hard at first, messy in the
middle and gorgeous at the end.

—Robin Sharma

During this time of deep soul searching and finding treasures that were spilling over into my life, my husband and I had drifted further and further apart. We were now living in different worlds, each world holding different sights and sounds and neither even closely resembling the other. One evening after work, I went to his barn to check in. The conversation was casual and surface. Later, as we walked together into the house, he continued out the other door. He stopped, turned, and told me he had moved out that day, taking all of his belongings to the cottage we owned next door.

While shocked, I also felt a sense of great relief. The last couple of years had been filled with constant pressure and stress, as there had been little more than constant criticism, blame, and judgment, and the house felt filled with fear and anger. With him now gone,

I knew that I could settle into a home filled with peace, where I could rest and recuperate from the stress that was always with me. While I did, he was next door waiting for me to come over and beg him to come home, to make the promises he wanted me to make and change in the ways he wanted me to change, and to be who he wanted me to be. It was too late, as I had finally found who I am, and there was no turning back. To do so would be pure emotional and mental suicide, and I had no wish to die to who I now knew that I am.

The path that I had been on, the path of self-delusion and bondage, was now coming to an end. My path was now leading me to truth and a taste of the freedom I had sought for so long. Ahead of me, I saw that a choice must be made. This path was over, and it was time to choose right or left. The choice was mine to make. Mentally standing in place for a while, a long while, confused in my own mind, I made no move.

Finally knowing a decision had to be made, I turned to the One who had led me this far, the One who knows, and I asked for wise guidance in my choice. In hearing no clear answer, I knew it was time to follow my heart for once. Finally, I chose right, to wait, still hoping for a miracle that would turn this situation around and having faith that whichever path I chose, I would be led along the way.

Again, my husband helped show me the way. He prided himself on being a doer, disdainfully calling me simply a thinker, never taking into account how powerful we could have been by combining our two strengths of doing and thinking things through before plowing forward—something I had been long hoping for. After a year, he gave me a choice, telling me it had been a year since he had moved out of our home and he felt he had given me enough time to make a decision regarding our relationship. Either I would take him back on his terms, or he would file for a divorce.

There was no choice. I knew I could not, would not take him back, as nothing had changed. Throughout this year, my hope had been to finally talk, communicate, and begin to repair the bridge that had been left in disrepair for so long. This never happened. He had no desire to repair; nor did he see a need for change. For him, it was to go back to how we had been long ago, into the memories he held most dear, or he was dissolving the relationship completely. We had come to the end of the path, and I was now given an ultimatum. Little did he know, it was an ultimatum I was thankful for. Living at the end of the path I had been on had not been peaceful. Even with my hope still strong, that hope was slowly eroding. And in my heart, I knew there would be no repair, no going back but only the final destruction of the fragile bridge we had managed to make in the past. The ax was out. The final blow was in front of me. I was ready.

He filed, still telling me that there was time to stop the divorce, if only I changed. Inwardly, I laughed. I was changing all right, right before his eyes, but not in the way he wanted me to change—not *his* way.

There was one thread of hope in my heart, and I again reminded him that we hadn't repaired what had caused the rift between us to grow so wide, and without repair, there was no us. This was not what he wanted to hear. He made the decision to sell two of our properties and called a realtor and then called me at work to let me know that the realtor would be out the next day. His voice was shaking and constricted, his fear evident.

When he hung up, I was emotionally thrown into a literal state of panic. It wasn't for fear of losing the properties, but I felt his pain, felt his fear, and compassion welled up in me so strong it threatened to overtake me. My thoughts rapidly turned to how I could heal his pain, calm his fear. Questioning my own decisions, I asked myself if I was moving in the right direction or living in a la-la land of illusions and make-believe; I questioned my own faith and love for the truth I had been seeking.

Suddenly, one word came to my mind—*empath*. It was like a slap across the face of my inner hysteria, and I immediately felt calm, realizing what was happening. I had absorbed his pain and fear, mistaking it as my own. Again thinking rationally, I knew I had not caused his fear and pain, any more than I could control the thoughts and emotions of anyone, other than my own. This experience led me to more truth about myself.

Throughout my life, empathy and compassion had been strong and always in the forefront of my decisions. This experience with my husband had shown me, once again, the strength of my empathy and compassion. Suddenly I saw how I had used these gifts to harm myself. In a sudden flashback of the past, I again saw that I had done this all my life. Worms in the playground. Oranges left alone in the grocery store and crying out to me. Cats rescued until I was overwhelmed. Hurting, wounded men I had rescued, who had fought to retain their freedom to be who they chose to be, cutting and wounding me in the process. My decisions in life had never been to fulfill my heart's call or desires but to help and please others, all in my attempt to heal them, with total disregard for myself. Would I choose to carry on this legacy of always saving others, allowing my own misled acts of compassion to dictate the steps of my life, with no thought for my own feelings, my own life? Being truthful with myself, I had to ask, Where has this gotten me? Into my own self-made hell, always feeling lost, unsatisfied, and resentful with no hope of change.

Within this insight, I could see that I had actually hurt others by this disregard for my own self. My disregard for my own truth hurt my mother by my acceptance of her desire for my life, instead of my own dreams, later to rebel against all she stood for. It had hurt my first husband because I'd married him simply to please another who held great importance in my life. And it had hurt my current husband because I'd allowed him to override all I wanted, desired, and dreamed of, so that I did not stand in the way of what he wanted, desired, and dreamed of.

This insight wasn't done, and I saw more. I saw that I had carried the guilt I was raised with to keep myself in place, doing nothing and going nowhere, stagnant in my self-made pit of quicksand that had made every attempt to pull me under. This all happened at once, and it was staggering yet freeing at the same time. Now I knew that I must learn to use this compassion wisely. Compassion is the essence of the Most High, but it was not meant to be used to torment my own *Self*! Compassion was in my heart to move me forward in setting the captive free, including me!

As this situation was new territory for me, with all the years, time, and money I had put into this marriage, now with properties involved, I needed some guidance, so I counter filed. As I drove away from picking up the divorce papers, I asked myself why I had waited so long. The answer came quickly. The rebel has a motto. "I don't give up! I can *do* this!" Recognizing this, I saw the energy it had taken to keep me in place, fighting a losing battle, unhappy, unsatisfied, and allowing myself to be emotionally beaten and abused by both my husband and myself. All wasted energy. Going forward, I must listen and chose my causes more wisely.

Just as suddenly, I caught a glimpse of the child in my past, who was not allowed to make decisions of her own, taught to obey and be a "good girl." I saw that I had been a good girl in this relationship, obeying the decisions made for my life that resulted, time and again, in so much work, every ounce of income, and emotional pain. My dutiful obedience had been a continual repeat of the past, bringing me no pleasure, no happiness. Now knowing my life did not have to be this way, I could walk away with rich treasures of lessons learned and truths obtained, and I was thankful.

In moving forward, I determined to use my life's energy, which is strong and powerful, for a greater cause than struggling to merely survive. I would devote this energy to truly living, living for myself, and use it wisely for others. I would stop wasting so much energy on fighting *against* something and use this energy to stand *for* something, for Truth, promoting the good of all, myself included!

There are a lot of teachings available these days about living in the now. This never made sense to me. My "now" seemed full of chaos and turmoil, questions, doubts, fears, and choices to be made. But a seed had been planted and was growing even though I was unaware. In truth, I had already made the decision to be happy *now*, but I did not relate this decision to living *in* the now. Yet, it was in the now that I could see what a cesspool I was living in, filled with dark, murky, poisonous thoughts, words, and actions that, if I had remained, would have killed me, just as I was beginning to finally live. Now, I was thankful that my husband had filed for divorce, as I was determined to remain, trying to bring back to life that which had already died. So, while there was turmoil as my world was being turned upside down, I recognized that I was beginning to see right side up! Instead of destruction, I was starting to see that, within this upheaval, the ground was being tilled and softened, and new beginnings could begin to sprout here and now.

Seeing all of this, many of my doubts and fears began to vanish. I saw that, in every now of every day, I had the opportunity to make new choices, decisions that benefitted me and my greatest desires. I had a change in perspective, looking at now in a new way. Why should I care about what happened in the past? The past was over, gone, and done with, and the only way I could relive it was if I brought it with me into my current now with my thoughts alone, which is what I had been doing all my life. There was no way I wanted to continue doing that! I would let the past stay back there where it belonged, as I had already learned much by looking at it. Today was a new day, presenting new choices and new opportunities to enjoy the life I truly desired to have!

Did I think about my future? Oh yes! I was walking away from supposed security, comfort, and a sure income for the rest of my life, which I'd have if I stayed right where I was and was willing to deny myself to please another. Yet, I was growing stronger, surer in my own strength and power to create for myself security, comfort, and an income that served me well. And now the future held no fear.

So I let the thoughts of the future go, knowing that, when I get there, I will be ready, capable, and prepared. I had enough to do right now and didn't want to waste energy on worrying about what may be or may never be in the days ahead! There was no need to remember where I had been or where I "might" be in the future, but who I am right here, right now! This realization brought great joy. I felt peace, like a heavy weight had been lifted, and I stepped further into true freedom.

Chapter 21

LOGJAMS: STILL FINDING MY WAY

Row, row, row your boat gently down the stream ...
merrily, merrily, merrily, merrily, life is but a dream.

—children's nursery rhyme

This simple little rhyme had been echoing over and over in my mind for many years. With the divorce now final and the house we shared sold, I felt settled and comfortable in my new home and gently rowing. Life was rolling peacefully down the stream, as I continued to listen and began to apply what I heard. As I did, my thoughts were changing. I felt at peace with myself and with life.

Then, logjams suddenly seemed to be appearing before me. Where were they coming from and why? What was their purpose? They were nothing that was actually occurring as events or situations but thoughts that keep rising up and standing in my way. I was starting to get angry; it appears it was time for a lesson in patience.

The lesson started out slowly, as what I was about to learn was new and different to my thinking. I was given a vivid analogy to help me see what is happening. It began with a picture of someone building a toy house out of blocks. The house was just about done, but there was one piece that didn't seem to fit. In a tantrum of impatience, the builder knocked the whole house down even though it was so close to perfection. If, instead of becoming frustrated, the builder had been patient, sat back, relaxed, and asked for guidance and another set of eyes to see through, before long, she would have seen where the piece fit, and the house would then be complete and whole.

At this time, while happy with my new life and freedom, I was busy thinking ahead to what came next and moving out of peace and into impatience. Now was not the time to think about what may or may not be ahead and start rowing my boat furiously to the next adventure; it was time to simply relax and enjoy what I now had. While I could see this clearly, I was to find it was easier sung than done. There was more I had to see.

These logjams and boulders appearing in my life seemed to be pieces that were left in my thinking that I didn't know where to put in the life I was creating, much like the toy house. Yet I felt they belonged somewhere to make my life whole. They were in my life for a reason, and I needed to see why to understand what I was to know and how to make the best use of them. So with a sigh, I asked and waited to see, to understand, and to know what to do. The answers began to appear as I tried patiently to wait.

Long before the divorce and all that occurred afterward, I was sure that, once I was settled in my new home, away from the chaos and distractions, I would quickly finish this book that I now called Ours. It wasn't just mine, as, while I shared my adventures, it was Spirit who had shown me the truth within each and every one of them. But once alone, with so much time to fill, I found that I was struggling to finish this book and send it on. Instead of the joy of finding my freedom while simply journaling, I had become bored with the editing, rewriting, and looking again and again at the past. I wanted something fun, something new and exciting that was not filled with the past. With these thoughts running through my mind, I was reminded that this book was not just about me; rather, it was guided by truth to help set those in pain and fear free. Instead of the thrill I normally felt hearing this Voice, I felt resentful and resistant. I dug in my heels and said out loud, "This book was *your* idea, not mine." And once again, throwing a tantrum, I thought, *You can't tell me what to do, and I'm taking a break.*

I just chose to quit listening. What I didn't realize at the time was that, in resisting, I was wandering away from the anchor that had been holding me safely in place, keeping me from being swept away into the swirling waters of fear and turmoil where logs and boulders could begin to appear, blocking my way.

Choosing to go my own way, I filled my time with meeting friends, going out, and having fun. And while I was enjoying myself, it wasn't long before I felt unsettled and uneasy and knew something was off kilter. And I knew exactly what it was. It was time to stop resisting and surrender to the task at hand and, even more, to start listening again, for it was only then that I felt centered and whole in peace. It was time to just accept and allow the stream to take me where I was meant to be going, and I knew I could not do this alone. Once again, I returned to listening to the gentle yet strong Voice within me.

Resuming my work, listening once more to Spirit's Voice, I was reminded again of why I was told to write it in the first place. Why waste all these years? Why throw the experiences away as nothing, when sharing all that I had lived—the knowledge and wisdom I had gained and the understanding that came from all the experiences I had chosen in my life—might help another find his or her own truth? All I had to do was share myself, open myself wide open to be seen and heard—something I had *never* done, even with those closest to me!

Suddenly, I am struck with intense fear! To purposely expose myself, naked and vulnerable, without the costume, the pseudo-image I had worn so long, to share my whole life, a life I'd kept hidden from everyone for so many years was a huge logjam! All my life I'd protected myself by not sharing myself with others, sharing only what I believed others wanted to see and hear. Yet I knew I'd been led to this very place where I'd been shown that love is always honest, always truthful. It was time to stop hiding behind fear and share what I'd experienced, where I'd gone. There are others like me who had wandered this same path all alone. It was time to throw off the fear and the guilt, both of which had chained me far too long from being who I am, and choose to be free. Did I dare? Yes, I was willing, as it was really, truly past time to forgive myself!

The logjam of fear and resistance didn't retreat for long as my thoughts turned again toward the future. Changes were coming, and what if I didn't like these changes? What if they pushed me too quickly out of my comfort zone and into the unknown? What if I was put in a place where I was expected to do and be what others wanted me to do and be? What if, what if, what if kept running through my mind, and I slammed the brakes on *hard*! But as I was beginning to discover, comfort and reassurance were not long in coming.

While I was digging in my heels in firm resistance by imagining I would be told how to live my life, I was asked if I really believed that I would be taken kicking and screaming somewhere I did not want to be. Again, I was reminded that I had every right to say yes or no to every request—that I did not have to submit to every demand. And who was to say that any of this would happen anyway?!

As I listened, suddenly I started laughing. All right already! Stop with fear-filled imaginings and start remembering who I AM and that I can say yes and I can say no. I do not have to do what anyone else wants me to do, but I am free to do what is best for me. Here I was resisting the future when I didn't even know what it is! My thoughts were what kept blocking my way, and it was time for me to take charge and move them firmly out of my way and just allow myself to continue to be led gently down the peaceful stream of life to exactly where I was to be.

A little rhyme came to my mind. "Round and round thoughts go, where they end up is under my control." And I, again, laughed out loud! As if that wasn't enough reassurance, right then I suddenly remembered a quote by Tony Robbins: "Stop being afraid of what could go wrong and start getting excited about what could go right!" Oh, Spirit is *so* good, bringing to my mind just the words I needed to hear!

This flow to true freedom did not stop there. Another logjam lay ahead. One night, in the midst of self-criticism, judgment, and disgust, I asked, "Why did it take me so long to learn?!" The response was quick and loud! Rapidly, I was informed that I did not come here to learn! I came here *knowing*, and there was nothing for me to learn except to learn how to stop resisting and allow myself to remember what I had forgotten. I was to remember that I had come here to have an adventure, to have fun, to experience things I'd never experienced before, and to know that I can have and I can be whatever I think that I can have and be.

In that moment, I was pulled out of despair and self-disgust, as this put a totally different slant on things. It was a new way of seeing life differently, taking the pressure off. I asked myself, Why *not* just have fun?! Why not view life as one grand adventure, filled with exciting moments and enjoyment? From that moment on, I saw life from a different perspective. And as my view of life changed, my life began to change, and my confidence grew. My trust expanded, and my world seemed filled with light and love and laughter. It became easy to laugh, as I found pleasure in everything I encountered. It seemed to open my ears to hear a word, a comment that brought laughter bubbling up and out, even shocking me as I heard myself, as laughter had never come easy for me. Others began commenting on my laughter, telling me how good it made them feel. Just a laugh was enough to share happiness with others. Later, I would be told that laughter charges the inner battery and makes our light shine bright. Oh yes, life *is* good, and I was here to enjoy it all!

In the meantime, my ex-husband and I had been talking, sharing, and going over the past and what had happened. We were beginning to see what I had resisted and what he had resisted to take us to the point of no return. He shared with me that, throughout all that had happened, he had been watching and began to see how centered and strong I really was and how I had focused on trusting the future to unfold as it would. My strengths were appearing, and I was discovering a new confidence never before experienced. And he had been observing all of this. We had amazed everyone around us with how closely we had worked together throughout the divorce and the sale, continuing to talk and support each other with every step. With this new space between us, we had both stopped resisting, stopped warring against each other to prove who was right and who was wrong, and it was easier to see what we hadn't seen before.

This new sight was having a profound effect on how my ex-husband was beginning to see himself, as well. Now alone, having achieved all he had set out to do, he was doing his own life review and asking himself the questions that would soon change who he thought he was. It was like watching a replay of what I had gone through a few years before. With our conversations becoming stimulating, revealing, and impactful, we were drawing closer than we had ever been before. There was now a peace and a trust between us. The logjams to truth had been removed and we were flowing forward into whatever life would hold for each of us.

As I review my life, I see the resistance that I was constantly clinging to. Instead of rowing my boat gently, surrendering to the flow, I was always paddling furiously upstream, making both my life and the lives of those around me difficult. That old "you can't tell me what to do" had bitten me over and over again, causing me to snap and snarl at others who I thought had been trying to control my life. The willingness to surrender has been difficult for me to achieve, as I had fought all of my life, thinking that I must fight or be imprisoned forever. These false thoughts were the darkness I was seeing through, and all appeared sinister, threatening, hiding the light within me, which is the truth of who I am.

When I made the choice to let my inner light shine, the darkness began to disappear. I began to see what was truly before me—what had always been there for me to see—and what beauty I saw. Finally, I could allow myself to stop the fighting, the resisting. As I did, my own self-image changed, how I saw all those who had been, and now were, in my life changed, what was occurring in the world around me changed; and it was all good, all pure, all truth, and lovely. Everyone who had been in my life had been instrumental in moving me forward to where I had come to be. None had been holding me back or holding me down but, rather, toughening me up; making me confident, strong, and resilient; and sharing lessons that I needed to learn to remember who and what I am and why I was here!

What an experience, what an adventure, what a life I'd lived—all with the help of all the parts of me that were here for me all along in others! With new sight, seeing a new life, I *loved* my life and all it had entailed and looked forward to the remaining time I chose to be here, seeing life for what it truly is—a beautiful, heavenly experience!

How many logjams must one encounter before finding an easy, simple way home to truth? Throughout this journey, I'd discovered that there were many and all within my own thoughts. But I'd been shown there is a different way to look at this. For every logjam, every boulder that I encountered, finding the way around, over, and through each one was only making me stronger and more confident in both myself and the guidance that I received. They were removing all the weak areas that used to leave me without the strength to move ahead.

In trust, I now knew that the way ahead will be made smooth, no matter what logjam I encounter, as I just patiently continue building my trust in the truth that life is good—when I stop resisting and allow it to be. So, back in my boat, I continue to merrily row down the healing stream of life, enjoying the scenery and trusting the current Who leads and guides me.

Chapter 22

TO BE OR NOT TO BE: THE ONLY CHOICE

*The good news of truth is joy ... say then from
the heart that you are the perfect day and
within you dwells the light that never ends.*

—The Gospel of Truth

*F*rom the dark, swirling chaos, the words were spoken. "Let there be light." And in this light, clarity dawned; who I thought I was died, to rise from the dead, reborn into the truth of who I am but had forgotten. Finding my true self was so easy, yet it appeared so difficult in the darkness of my chaotic thoughts. It was in finally listening to the pain within me—this pain that had been within me for the entirety of my life, its cries becoming louder and louder with each day until it drowned out all other sounds—that I was at last led to where the pain had always tried to take me. I was taken home to the truth, found in the light. Whereas once I was without, now I am within, where the truth abides. I can lay aside all the tears, the suffering, the wrongs, the rights, the shoulds, the shouldn'ts, the judgment, and the condemnation and just rest in the peace of simply being who I am.

When I really stopped to look for myself and found the real me, then recognition dawned; self-acceptance replaced self-rejection; and my heart could live, beating strong. It is a beautiful thing to surrender what is not real, to remember only that which is real. Rumi wrote, "The cure for pain is in the pain." I have found this to be true.

Too often we blame people and circumstances, but those outer things cannot hurt us when we know who we truly are. For most of my life, pain is all I held within my thoughts, and it worked like a magnet, drawing pain to me, as this is what I knew and was familiar with. In return, I gave pain, as it was what I knew and had been taught to give. It is true that "hurt people hurt people." Do we mean to? *Oh no!* We are only giving of what seems real to us, which is pain.

The sages throughout time tell us that we can "learn through joy or through pain." It appears that I chose the latter, for I have experienced much pain and have given much as well. Yet, pain's voice is loud and will lead us to truth and joy if we but listen and follow where pain's voice is taking us. In looking back, I wonder if I had been so rebellious that I would not listen to joy's voice, for joy is easy, light, and carefree. Or maybe I just could not understand joy's voice, because it was unfamiliar, strange, and like nothing I had ever known. It took pain, something that I was familiar with, to get through to me—to push me hard enough that I finally rebelled against the pain and turned in the other direction to finally find myself on track to the joy I'd never known.

It was in finally understanding that I did not need to change who I am but, rather, just change who I mistakenly thought I was— the thoughts and beliefs that held me back—that I obtained true vision and I really, truly liked who I finally saw. The heavy load I had been carrying was lifted, and the freedom I had always sought was finally mine to have. This burden was not physical but mental and emotional, images I had formed from words spoken with only my vivid imagination leading me forward into a world created by my thoughts alone. Now I know there was no truth in the words I'd heard in the past, but I had accepted them just the same and made them my reality.

Life is such a simple mind game, a game that can be changed at any time we choose. Yet, first, we must see that we are playing a game that only we can change. It was in finding truth that I could finally see. Truth is this bright, beautiful, brilliant light that is always radiating through and around us, but with closed eyes, we cannot see it. Now, with eyes wide open, it was like being a little child again, full of wonder and excitement, amazed at each new discovery. And I found it all by asking for help and being willing to follow the guidance I was given to look back and find what I had lost, which was my true self.

It was here, at the end of this story, that I did one more quick review and found it so simple, yet seemingly so difficult at the time. It was in finally understanding that the thoughts I had been given from conception had formed beliefs. These beliefs had formed my self-perception, which had then formed the judgments I held against myself. It was in choosing to look, and finally seeing, that I was free and could remove my own self-judgment. Once I did, the judgments I held against others just disappeared. As they did, forgiveness came easy, as, with no judgment, I saw there was nothing to forgive anyone for. Here, I landed smack-dab into freedom and peace, with new eyes, new ears, true thoughts, and a new life. Shaking my head, I once again wondered how I could have ever believed these thoughts in the first place. But this wonder was quickly replaced with the truth that I'd simply forgotten what I knew before I came to believe I was someone other than who I am. It was like waking up from a bad nightmare and heaving a huge sigh of relief in realizing the nightmare wasn't even real, and I was safe and right where I belonged—in the arms of Love, where I had always been and will forever be.

The transformation in my life is proof to me of a power greater than any that appears to walk this earth. It is a power that transcends the human mind with all of its amazing abilities, reasoning, and human knowledge to reveal a very simple truth that I am love, I am loved, and I am here to love—nothing more, nothing less. With the powers that try to control through societal, religious, and cultural hypnosis and brainwashing, this appears to be a monumental feat to overcome, a task impossible to achieve. But take a look within and find that the difficult can be made easy and the impossible just takes a little longer. All we have to do is get out of our own way and stop trying to control what we cannot control. Like they say in Alcoholics Anonymous, "Let go and let God."

It has been this Sword of Truth, wielded by Spirit, that cut this captive free. Now, I know it will be with me always, continuing to cut away whatever binds and blinds me, so that I will see the truth in the days ahead. The insane thoughts of the world had ruled my life long enough. I have found this prison made of thoughts distasteful, painful, and filled with fear. And I am ready to be free. All it took was the sacrifice of false thoughts for true, the only sacrifice I was asked to make. Yet, can giving up what has no value be a sacrifice? To give up fear for peace, captivity for freedom, and hate for love is no sacrifice. Rather, it's an offering willingly made. It is all we are asked to do—to make the choice to be willing.

Ralph Waldo Emerson wrote, "We ask for long life, but 'tis deep life, or grand moments that signify." While I have never given much thought to how long I will live, I now know that I have lived a deep life in many ways by exploring the depths of human experience in realms many never dared enter. Now, I am ready to explore more, as there are many things I have not experienced in my life. The depth of living knows no bounds, and there are grand adventures that lie ahead. With nothing behind me that binds me to the past and my future unknown, I have the present moment to enjoy, to be fully present now, and to receive the truth that life so willingly gives. No longer caring what others think or what they believe, I know that life is for me. I travel free to explore the yet unknown that is calling to me. What can possibly be better than this?!

Within these pages, I have only shared less than half of my life's experiences. Perhaps I will share more another time. Perhaps not. For now, I am ready to let the past rest in peace, enjoy the present of the moment, and look forward to a new life of truth ahead.

With this, I close this story for now, as there is a new story to write about a new life, new beginnings, and new adventures. Yet, I do not close the door on all that I have experienced in the past, as I now have a better understanding of the many paths there are to choose from and what is along these paths to be seen. My experiences have given rise to a deep compassion for all who travel, and I can now say this to everyone—never give up, never turn back in despair, keep on keepin' on. And you, too, will reach the place you seek for the truth will set you free!

One final gift I wish to give is the words to "Sweet Surrender" by John Denver, a song that, for me, sings the song of truth:

> Lost and alone on some forgotten highway, traveled by many, remembered by few, looking for somethin' that I can believe in, looking for somethin' that I want to do with my life. There's nothin' behind me and nothin' that ties me to something that might have been true yesterday. Tomorrow is open and right now it seems to be more than enough to just be here today. I don't what the future is holding in store, I don't know where I'm going, I'm not sure where I've been. There's a Spirit that guides me, a Light that shines for me, my life's worth the living, I don't need to see the end. Sweet, sweet surrender.

Live, live without care like a fish in the water, like
a bird in the air.

And now, I am on my way and bid you a final adieu, wishing
you happiness, contentment, and the fulfillment found only in
truth. May these words reach those who are seeking, as I did. And
may you find the way to the peace and freedom just waiting to be
found in finding the truth of who we are. Thank you for traveling
this journey with me, and I wish you happy travels of your own.
Namaste—the truth in me sees the truth in you!

Conclusion

Every morning I am born again. What
I do today is what matters most.

—Buddha

Writing this story took several years. As my thoughts changed, which was daily, I went back to continually rewrite my story in an attempt to remove anything I had written that made me appear as a victim to the life I lived or blaming others instead of taking responsibility for myself. This occurred too many times until I finally saw that this *is* my story. Mine is a story of transformation—from thinking I was a victim to finding the truth that I am a victor—finally seeing truth, knowing at last that I could change my whole life story, the past, the present, and what may come in my future. The truth was that I am in control, have always been in control and that no one can hurt me, stop me, shame me, or delay me any longer from being who I truly am—the real me that I came here to be. I did this by asking the question, "What if ... I'm not real?" Questions will open doors to answers from One who knows.

Where life takes us is often funny, and in looking back, we see how we got to where we are today. When we can look at the past with laughter, it seems to change the whole picture. There have been times that I have questioned why I chose the rutted, bumpy road that I did, and the answer is simple when explained. It was because I can see more along my travels. Laughing, I understood, as I still choose the back roads versus the highway whenever I possibly can. Why choose the boring route when I can take the exciting scenic route along the way, see and smell the flowers and experience the, as yet, unknown?! It is all good, all leading to truth, in whatever way we choose. Here, at this end and onto a new beginning, I find myself laughing most of the time, and it feels good. This feel-good feeling increases when I know that I'm not done and can look forward to what is ahead.

The me that I made with my own thoughts was a fake, an imposter who had been walking around in my place. Having made the choice to leave the imposter behind, I can proceed on as I truly am. There is freedom in this choice and a peace that passes all understanding that I wouldn't trade for all the riches of the world. As I reached the end of this story, I stopped the futile attempts to separate past, present, and future and just enjoyed living here now, in this moment, and simply being.

To find our true self is to be reborn, turning weakness into strength, fear into power, and darkness into the Light by which we see. In this world, from the time we are born, we are taught to make life difficult by dividing everything into separate sections, where we see past, present, and future; that I am separate from you and you from me; and that life is a struggle as we try to make it on our own. This is not true living, as with no backup, no teamwork, we land flat on our face and find no one there to help us up. What a lonely, scary life we are taught to live all alone.

To find the truth is to find that we are all in this together, none of us is ever separate, and it is never about each individual part finding the way alone. Seen in truth's Light, we see we are all holding hands, all heading in the same direction and all seeking the way back to the land of peace, harmony, love, and happiness. When we find this truth, believe it and know it, we join as One, holding each other up; lifting each other when we falter and start to fall; sharing each other's victories and mistakes; and comforting, encouraging, and cheering each other on. This is when the way becomes so much easier. Joined as One, when one finds the Light, the Light is shared by all so that all can see. When we can clearly see where our steps are taking us, our steps become braver, stronger, and longer, and we all get to where we are going that much sooner. When we know we are never alone, we hold the hands of those around us, walking in the Light of Truth, with clear direction, joined purpose, laughing together and excited to be headed home. Like Dorothy lost in the Land of Oz, we know there is no place like home. So, holding hands, we just click our heels and find ourselves there—together—forever as One, right here, right now.

Remember what matters and remember I am you, you are me, and we are all One in the One Who is known as Love.

Acknowledgments

There are many I would like to "point the finger at" and say, "You did this!" And then I'd give them a huge hug of gratitude and love! I will just mention a few here, all in random order. Briefly within these pages, I have mentioned the billboards; the quotes heard on television; and the words spoken by those I know, those I have momentarily met, and even strangers. All have been my teachers and have shared truth with me in one form or another. I thank them all. When the heart is open, the gifts are seen, received, and appreciated.

Heal Your Body by Louise Hay—This book transformed my life, and I have carried a copy in my purse for almost thirty years. The wisdom in this "little blue book" has helped keep me healed and whole and has shown me much about others who I meet, as by their sickness and dis-ease I have learned their thoughts.

Medicine Cards by Jamie Sams and David Carson—This book opened the door to the wisdom in all of creation and taught me how to listen and hear the ancient truth spoken in nature and by the animals who share this world with us. Through using this book, I met my totem, Hawk, who has taught me to always be alert, aware, and observant of the messages of truth all around and within me. A deep appreciation of my Mother Earth and all she provides now abides in my heart.

The Bible—This ancient book first stirred within me as a young child the need to question. These questions would never leave me and would prompt me my whole life to seek truth. Later, also while reading, I first heard the Voice that told me, "God is love. If it isn't love, it isn't God"—words that have never left my heart and continue to echo in my mind. Reading it still to this day, I am being shown that, to live the life we are here to live, we must follow the example of Jesus and allow the Spirit of Love to speak words of truth through us to heal and raise the dead of those sick in mind, to lift the poor out of their poverty, and to uphold and protect the innocent—to affect the very world around us by turning our voice over to the One who knows the truth. Not my will, but Yours be done.

A Course in Miracles—Over twenty years ago, I "accidently" stumbled on a webinar taught by Marianne Williamson teaching on the Course. Her words so moved me that I bought the book and the full set of cassette tapes that sat on my shelf for the next fifteen years unopened. The day came when this student was ready, and the teacher was there patiently waiting for me to begin to learn.

My parents—Through their actions, and inaction, they taught me how to be self-sufficient, how to enjoy the pleasure of my own company, and the wonders found in silence. Through them, I eventually learned to stand up and defend my right to be and the error of living another's will for my life, as it only leads to a life of misery and pain. Through it all, love was always there.

My last husband—He is the one who contracted with me before time began to give and receive the lessons we both came to learn. He was my mirror, reflecting back to me how I saw myself and the one who finally pushed me to the edge to take the leap and find the one I'd lost—who I truly am. We were both surprised at who I found.

To those noted here and many more, I give my heartfelt thanks and eternal love.